Treasure Craft Pottery & Pottery Craft Stoneware

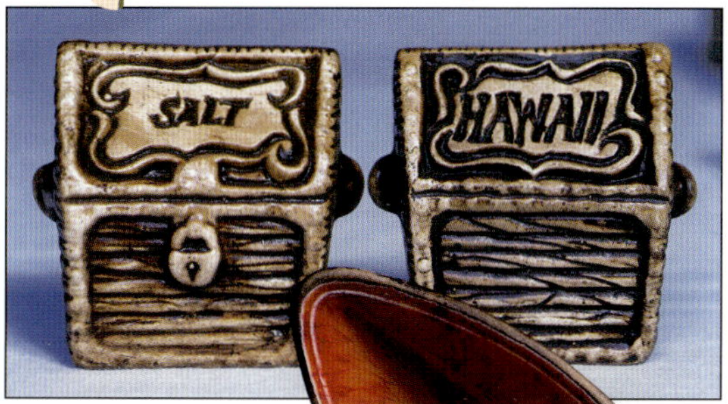

George A. Higby, ISA

Schiffer Publishing Ltd

4880 Lower Valley Road, Atglen, PA 19310 USA

This book is dedicated to

Alfred Levin
1915-1995

without whom Treasure Craft—and this book—would never have been

Copyright © 2004 by George A. Higby, ISA
Library of Congress Control Number: 2004102484

    All rights reserved. No part of this work may be reproduced or used in any form or by any means—graphic, electronic, or mechanical, including photocopying or information storage and retrieval systems—without written permission from the publisher.
    The scanning, uploading and distribution of this book or any part thereof via the Internet or via any other means without the permission of the publisher is illegal and punishable by law. Please purchase only authorized editions and do not participate in or encourage the electronic piracy of copyrighted materials.
    "Schiffer," "Schiffer Publishing Ltd. & Design," and the "Design of pen and ink well" are registered trademarks of Schiffer Publishing Ltd.

Designed by Mark David Bowyer
Type set in Dom Bold BT/Humanist 521 BT

ISBN: 0-7643-2072-6
Printed in China
1 2 3 4

Published by Schiffer Publishing Ltd.
4880 Lower Valley Road
Atglen, PA 19310
Phone: (610) 593-1777; Fax: (610) 593-2002
E-mail: Info@schifferbooks.com

For the largest selection of fine reference books on this and related subjects, please visit our web site at
www.schifferbooks.com
We are always looking for people to write books on new and related subjects. If you have an idea for a book please contact us at the above address.

This book may be purchased from the publisher.
Include $3.95 for shipping.
Please try your bookstore first.
You may write for a free catalog.

In Europe, Schiffer books are distributed by
Bushwood Books
6 Marksbury Ave.
Kew Gardens
Surrey TW9 4JF England
Phone: 44 (0) 20 8392-8585; Fax: 44 (0) 20 8392-9876
E-mail: info@bushwoodbooks.co.uk
Free postage in the U.K., Europe; air mail at cost.

Contents

Acknowledgments 4

Foreword 5

Who Collects Treasure Craft—and Why 6

Pricing Your Collection 9

Condition and the Care of Treasure Craft 11

In the Beginning... Gardena and South Gate, California: 1947-1955 ... 14

Transition to Compton: 1955-1959 34

Treasure Craft of Hawaii 49

The Promise of the 1960s 76

The 1970s: Decade of Change 97

Pottery Craft, USA 105

Big Successes in the Big '80s 117

The Pfaltzgraff Years: 1988-1995 138

Limited Edition Cookie Jars 148

How Treasure Craft Was Made 158

Marks and Labels 161

Look Alikes 166

Treasure Craft Alumni 172

Bibliography 174

Index 175

Acknowledgments

It's been fun and fascinating, but it was no easy feat to examine and understand the production of a firm as long-lived and varied as Treasure Craft. It took the help of many people to get a full view.

Some spent hours with me in interviews, offered catalogs, photos, and contacts; others lent items for photos, proofread, offered equipment, and places to stay. Whether the contribution was great or small, it all proved essential to making this book the best it could be, and I extend my heartfelt thanks to all:

Antique Journal; Ann Blackmore; "Blenko Bill" Agle; Mike and Doreen Booth; Mary Buckler; Jack Chipman; Centralia Square Antique Mall; Debbie and Randy Coe; Sheila Conant; Stephanie Conant; Bill Delisi; Gayle Chronister; Clarence and Audrey De Coite; Duane, Stacy, and Zach Drake; Stace Elliott and Elizabeth Dodson; James Elliott-Bishop and Patrick Barry; Mike Ellis; Jan Esterly; Tom Gorz; Milan Hagen; Bill Hamburg; Christine Heath; Sally Higby; Liz Janes-Brown; Carl Johansen; Georgie Johnston; Justice Designs; Jonathan and Deb Kelley; Connie Kettman; Jerry Labb and Cynthia Conrad; Lafayette School Antique Mall; David Lane; Bruce, Jeanette, and Jolene Levin; Susan Malysiak; Robert Maxwell; Mc Me Productions; Dave Miller; Old Stuff Magazine; Frances Nascimento; Pioneer Square Mall; Annette Psyck; Charles Powell; Becki Ray; John Regan; Grace Robinson; Mari-Lynn Romero; Schiffer Publishing; Reba Schneider; Snohomish Star Center Antique Mall; Dennis Snook and Carl Todd; Jeff Snyder; Brian and Laurel Spellman-Smith; Carlos Soto; Ellen Stonecypher; Sylvia Tompkins; Michael Walker and Taina Karr; 222 Westlake Antiques; Reina Windrum; Don Winton; George A. Woolsey, Jr.

…and extra thanks to countless unmentioned others who helped make this book possible.

Foreword
Treasure Craft—A Post-Mortem of American Industry

In 1989, George Higby, fresh out of the University of Washington, decided to take on the job of marketing our string of northwest antique malls. His work began in Snohomish, Washington, where we had converted an old armory building into the Star Center Antique Mall. George coordinated the publication of our in-house *Antique Quarterly* gazette, and produced advertising copy for Star Center, Centralia Square, and Oregon's Lafayette Schoolhouse antique malls.

Little did George know his career path would be interrupted by the dying gasps of some of America's best known manufacturers. In 1988, outerwear manufacturer London Fog approached me about opening a factory outlet store in Centralia. London Fog had produced outerwear in Eldersberg, Maryland, since the 1920s, but the competitive climate had become more difficult. Though traditional department stores like Nordstrom's carried London Fog, they often promoted higher margin, foreign made knockoffs with the department store label instead.

London Fog felt that if they could bypass the middleman and sell directly to the public, their Eldersberg facility could stay open and competitive. I agreed to build a factory outlet store facing I-5 in Centralia. At the time, I didn't realize how many other manufacturers were in the same position as London Fog.

With projected annual sales of $600,000, London Fog opened in February 1988. Within weeks of the opening, I received calls from manufacturers all over the East Coast wanting to come to Centralia. It seemed London Fog was telling other producers that Centralia was a success; first year sales totaled $3,600,000, a staggering $700 per square foot.

Overwhelmed with requests for store space from the likes of U.S. Shoe, Van Heusen, and Corning Glass, we began building more outlet stores. I called George for help, and he packed his bags and relocated to Centralia. We began a four-year project of building and marketing what became a forty-store outlet center. Our mission was to help save American manufacturing by marketing American-made goods direct to the consumer.

By 1991, we incorporated our business as Shopping Destinations, Inc., with George serving as Vice-President. The new firm encompassed five antique malls, the factory outlet mall, and a variety of related enterprises. We directly managed outlets for small manufacturers like Pilgrim Glass of West Virginia and Seattle's International News. We opened a Mount St. Helens glassblowing facility, and created the NW Factory Co-op to sell the goods of local manufacturers. Our factory outlet marketing emphasized "Made in America," while *Antique Quarterly* often featured stories of great American companies and the things they once made.

Pfaltzgraff, parent firm of Treasure Craft, decided to open an outlet in Centralia in 1991. Pfaltzgraff was a coveted tenant, rooted in America with 150 years of manufacturing in Pennsylvania. Centralia would be their first West Coast outlet store, and their executives boasted that there would never be foreign made goods sold in its outlets. Everything would be made in the U.S.A.!

During the early 1990s, a period of great debate arose among American manufacturers of apparel and household goods. The value of "Made in America" versus the lure of cheap offshore labor was a big question. Nike had proven that design and manufacturing need not be integrated in one place, but many argued that it was an exception.

The passage of the North American Free Trade Agreement (NAFTA) seemed to clinch the debate. Despite the protests of many American manufacturers, it was clear our country's trade policies had shifted to encourage American factories to move production across the border. Mexican and Central American free trade zones were set up to reduce production costs by giving American companies access to low cost labor in a virtually tax-free environment.

Until the 1990s, Treasure Craft designers worked alongside production workers in their Los Angeles plant. Post-NAFTA, production was contracted to factories in Mexico and China.

After NAFTA, manufacturers no longer discussed *whether* to move offshore, but *how*. Five years after our outlet center opened, "Made in America" was no longer meaningful to customers. Van Heusen, Corning, Farberware, London Fog, U.S. Shoe...almost all our tenants moved most (if not all) production out of the United States. Pfaltzgraff closed the Treasure Craft plant in California, replacing American made Treasure Craft pottery with inferior versions made in Mexico, then China. Then Treasure Craft was discontinued.

I recall a lunch with George in Centralia Square's Antique Mall Café in 1993. *USA Today* had run a feature about a big investment opportunity in factory outlet real estate investment trusts. We mused that by the time investment opportunities hit the news, it was usually too late. How could there be factory outlets when the factories were all closing?

In 1995, George became president of Shopping Destinations, but the company's goal was no longer expansion. "Made in America" marketing no longer worked, and outlet mall sales were falling. For three years, George sold or closed operating units of Shopping Destinations, returning our company to its roots, and opening another antique mall in Seaside, Oregon.

The closure of Treasure Craft marked the end of Southern California's 1940s pottery boom. In a larger sense, the closure marks a fundamental shift in the direction of many companies that were once American manufacturers. Success in the new world order meant shifting from a manufacturing focus to one of marketing. Some companies were unable to make this transition; Treasure Craft was one of them.

John Regan
Centralia, Washington
December, 2003

Who Collects Treasure Craft-and Why

Treasure Craft has been part of my environment since childhood, even though I didn't know it at the time. My grandma in San Diego had Sprites liberally sprinkled throughout her patio garden and planters. On our console sat a matador and bull, and my sister got half-a-dozen varieties of tropical leaf serving trays as wedding presents in 1971.

In the late 1980s, I spotted three of those flame-glazed leaf trays in a Goodwill store. A wave of nostalgia hit, and I took them home to proudly display on my sideboard. My next visitor pointed at them, shook her head in disbelief, and asked, "Why?".

At the time, it seemed a legitimate question. Their 1960s wood tones and psychedelic glazes stood in sharp contrast to the prevailing pastels and cool tones of the '80s, and their naturalistic design defied streamlined neo-deco. Treasure Craft was still in production, and little green Sprites and wood stain cookie jars were omnipresent in thrift stores.

A generation later, all that has changed. Last of the major California potteries, Treasure Craft is no more, and collectors have begun to salt away some of the thousands of items they made over a half-century of production. Writers of collector magazines and reference books have started to recognize Treasure Craft. And that same friend wants one of their hula dancers in the tight white dress…she looks just like her!

Treasure Craft Sprites, c. 1950: *Playful* (crawling) and *Happy* (seated), 2.75" x 3.75". Green, $15-18; red, $18-20.

Monstera leaf ashtray, red, c. 1960s, Hawaii, 12", $18-22.

Collecting Treasure Craft—Without Even Trying

Some collectors are joining me in amassing large groupings of Treasure Craft while it's still affordable and available. Many other pottery collections already include Treasure Craft pieces, without their owners even realizing it.

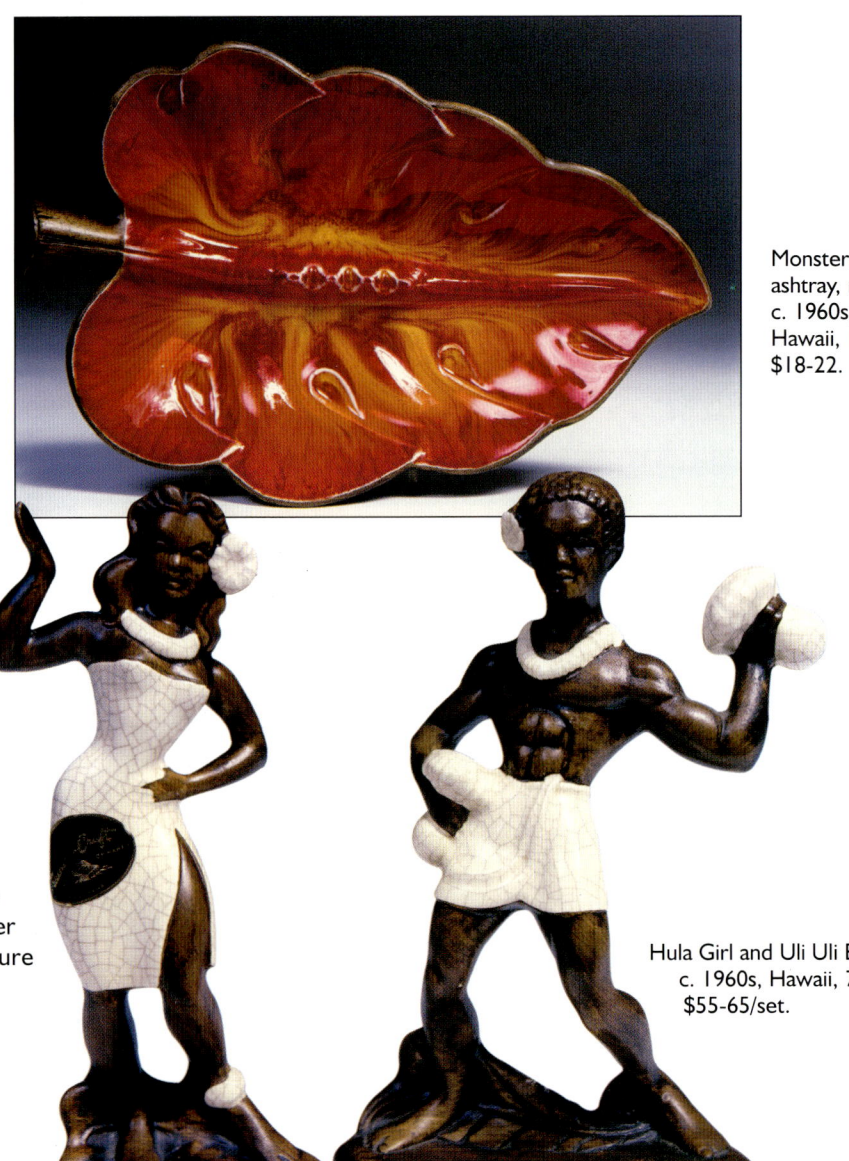

Hula Girl and Uli Uli Boy, c. 1960s, Hawaii, 7.5", $55-65/set.

Disneyana collectors often own Treasure Craft pieces sold at the theme parks (such as the Big Al Country Bear bank) or through department stores (like the scarce Simba cookie jar from the Lion King). Salt-and-pepper collectors point out favorite novelties like the Indian seated in the canoe or the 1940s car with trailer, unaware that their unmarked gems were made by the firm.

Hawaiiana is enjoying renewed collector fervor, and sinuous Treasure Craft hula dancers and fearsome tiki gods often anonymously appear in collector displays (and even the Tommy Bahamas™ catalog). Muscular dancer pairs, cowboys with stallions, and matadors with bulls are featured in homes of pottery collectors, loved for their design but without a trace of their origin.

Don Winton clay model for Mickey Mouse® phone stand, fired at Treasure Craft, c. 1977. Prototype (production models were made in plastic).

Paint can and brush shakers, c. 1940s, 2" and 3.25", $15-20.

Fish four-section tray, #390, peacock, c. 1960s, 17.5", $25-30.

Cookie jar fans often gather some of Treasure Craft's 200 novelty pieces and short-lived limited editions, not knowing that many more exist. *Wizard of Oz* fans prize the scarce character jar line, but rarely notice the maker's name in small print on the bottom. Many modern homemakers seek replacement pieces for their discontinued southwest-style dinnerware, enjoying it daily, but unaware that many other pieces exist.

Cookie Trolley, antique white, c. 1975, 9" x 11", $30-35.

Matador planter with box, experimental dark wood stain, 1958, 8", $18-20.

"Today's Gifts, Tomorrow's Heirlooms"

Treasure Craft's bombastic 1950s sales slogan may prove prophetic. As with other major American potteries, items made in large numbers for a mass market are proving familiar and desirable to large numbers of collectors. The legacy of those who brought the ware to households across North America endures.

For all these reasons, it seems timely to record and preserve the memory of the last of California's major pottery firms. My hope is that this book will inspire current collectors to grow their collections, show new collectors an exciting variety of pottery collectibles, and give credit to the people who designed and produced Treasure Craft for five decades.

Pricing Your Treasure Craft Collection

Besides learning more about your collection and discovering all there is to buy, part of the fun of a collector reference book is being able to estimate values on pieces you find!

As a collector, dealer, and appraiser, I believe in the importance of reliable, non-hypothetical pricing information. Reference book prices are only as valid as the methods used to establish them.

Stated values in this book reflect recent actual sales of comparable pieces of Treasure Craft and Pottery Craft. This follows from my training and accreditation through International Society of Appraisers, which compels us to certify that values we set reflect the true nature of the product and the market.

To reduce pricing anomalies, I've studied the market for Treasure Craft carefully over the past few years. For example, I first saw the Midnight Sun chip and dip sell for $136 in a live auction bidding war, yet it consistently sold since for $50-60. On the other hand, hearing someone say, "I saw the Lila Lamb cookie jar online for only $10!" discounts the $15 extra in shipping, insurance, and tracking it took to actually get it.

Naturally, no book can guarantee that prices realized in the past will reflect future values. This is only a guide, and as such, the author and publisher accept no liability for pricing or purchasing decisions made based on the values stated herein.

Santa in sleigh, c. 1953, 5.75" x 5.75", $45-55.

Leopard cookie jar, 1980s, 12.5", $45-55.

The sources of these values are as varied as the places Treasure Craft can be found. Antique shops, malls, and shows, online and live auctions, swap meets, used goods stores, and private sales are all sources of valuation I've studied in preparing this book.

Prices shown are based on the assumption that the item is in undamaged, original condition (even if the piece shown is not). Prices are generally expressed in a range, reflecting differences between regions, seasonal fluctuations, etc.

Zebra wall plaque, c. 1955, USA embossed mark, 11" x 20.75". This may be an early wood stained piece by Treasure Craft, but bears no foil label from the period. Value unknown.

What Will Future Values Be?

The outlook for Treasure Craft/Pottery Craft seems good. Publication of this book will increase awareness and collector interest, and some items will prove scarcer than originally thought. Collectors who follow the work of certain designers will discover that certain Treasure Craft wares fit their collections. New items will likely be discovered, perhaps to be shown (along with value updates) in a future edition of this book.

Treasure Craft should benefit as new generations join the collector ranks. Their 1940s and '50s figural wares already have adherents, while their 1960s and '70s pieces are starting to reach nostalgia seekers who came of age in those eras. Pottery Craft lines are beginning to find favor with collectors of the generically titled "Eames Era" modernism. And the depth and quality of Treasure Craft production in the 1980s and '90s will ultimately inspire pattern matchers and cookie jar fans to seek these lines as they slip farther back into history.

Robert Maxwell designed Pottery Craft stoneware vases, Tierra overlapping colors, c. 1975, 5.5"-6.5", $18-28/ea.

Condition and the Care of Treasure Craft

Discriminating pottery collectors naturally prefer pieces free of cracks, chips, scrapes, and repairs. A careful evaluation of Treasure Craft wares will help you choose wisely and protect your investment.

Keys to Judging Condition

Early Treasure Craft earthenware prospered against cheap imports by being lightweight and easy to ship. Fired at low temperatures, areas not sealed under a clear coat (such as Sprite faces, or Wood Stain rims) were simply varnished or painted. Careless use could easily scrape or chip them, and ammonia spray cleaners could remove finishes. Repainting or restaining of Sprite caps, Gnome faces, and fish tray fins was a common remedy, so pieces should be reviewed with a keen eye.

Since wood stained figurines were lacquered to seal them, their white crackle sections were imparted a mellow ivory cast, which varied in intensity depending on the decorator. Cleaning with abrasives often removed this, evidenced today by a glossy whiteness. (An artistic hand could acceptably restore this varnish, so the effect on current values has proven slight.)

A close look at this Wee Wun on leaf shows chips colored green by a prior owner. Circa 1950, 3" x 5", $15-20.

The original lacquer on this Flamenco woman was worn away by abrasive or ammonia cleaners.

Pricing Your Treasure Craft Collection

A greater problem is the bleaching of wood stain wares. Dishwashers would scour the brown stain, which was intended to be cleaned by hand. Another effect is a hazy whiteness in the brown, similar to driftwood found on a beach; this was a factory flaw caused by the efflorescence of moisture trapped in the lacquer spray. Primarily seen on Hawaiian items, it happened when items were sprayed on humid autumn days. At its best, the flaw gave faux wood pieces an interesting weathered look; at worst, it resulted in an unappealing grayish cast.

Dropped lids often left hidden cracks and chips on canisters or cookie jars. Metal ware could speckle when left damp for long periods, and even the rugged dinnerware and stoneware lines could scratch under a heavy hand.

For all these reasons, savvy collectors have learned to examine Treasure Craft in person, or buy only from a trusted online or mail order source. Of the dozens of pieces I've purchased online, an incredible one-in-four came with unnoticed damage, were smashed due to poor shipping procedures, never arrived, or were misrepresented! When shopping online, it is buyer beware, so I've trained myself to ask lots of questions, and specify packing requirements.

The whitewashed look of this Pirate mug was caused by moisture trapped under the lacquer seal coat, either during manufacturing or dish washing. Circa 1970, 7.25", $15-20.

Damage has proven to be an all too common result of online ordering. Before its destruction, this scarce c. 1955 Sprite on bear planter in tan would have sold for $50-60.

Care and Feeding of Your Treasure Craft

With just a little care, it's easy to enjoy Treasure Craft today, while preserving it for tomorrow.

Sprites, wall pockets, and planters are happy to live with plants, but should be lined to prevent lime stains. Vases should be cleaned and water changed or dumped between uses. Only indoor use is recommended.

Figurines can be safely held in place with Quake Hold © or Museum Gel ©. Wood Stain can be gently bathed in warm water with mild soap if needed, but less is more…occasional dusting (never rubbing or scrubbing) is preferable. Contrary to the instructions on Treasure Craft's hang tags, "waxing the finish like real wood" seems inadvisable, as examples treated that way now seem to bear an odd glossy sheen.

Contrasting colored glazes on Wood Stain pieces are protected by a clear overglaze, and can handle harder scrubbing if needed.

After 1975, most Treasure Craft was made to be safe in oven, dishwasher, and microwave. Cocinera chip and dip, two-section, 1980s, 12.5" and 5.5", $20-25.

Pottery Craft stoneware planters can be perfectly happy outdoors, but lining is again recommended so they don't calcify or crack under freeze/thaw conditions. Pottery Craft is dishwasher and oven safe; however, as with any ceramic ware, it's advisable to graduate temperatures and avoid such extremes as dunking a 350-degree casserole dish in cold water.

Most Treasure Craft made after 1975 matches today's desire for carefree, casual living, with low-maintenance earthenware protected by a clear coat. Microwave and dishwasher-safe, the dinnerware is well suited for everyday use; liquid soap won't abrade the clear overglaze like granular detergents. Cookie jars and tableware should only need an occasional wipe down to stay fresh for years.

With minimal attention, your Treasure Craft collection can be enjoyed every day for years to come.

Pottery Craft stoneware was cooked at around 2000 degrees Fahrenheit to be rugged and versatile. Tall face mug, Tierra, c. 1975, 7.5", $9-12.

Condition and the Care of Treasure Craft

In the Beginning... Gardena and South Gate, California: 1947-1956

Like his neighbors, Alfred Levin, his wife, and two babies lived in a modest two bedroom home in the sprawling new suburban tracts of Los Angeles. Unlike his neighbors, Levin's garage was home to a fledgling new enterprise, comprising the home office and shipping center of Treasure-Craft, Incorporated.

Pure happenstance led this native Chicagoan to the California pottery business. Born July 15, 1915 in Chicago to Irving and Bessie Levin, Al's youth was spent in an era of middle class prosperity—but he came of age in the uncertain depths of the Depression. Fortunately, he applied himself vigorously enough to qualify for further education after his high school years ended.

Now an amazingly spry octogenarian, Jeanette Levin noticed her husband-to-be in 1933 while both were attending a college psychology class at the Jewish People's Institute. "The professor would play word association games with Al, who was a quick wit. Al started offering to walk me home after study group, and we knew the first week it was right." Still, the couple waited to wed until their studies were completed, marrying May 1, 1938.

Early in their marriage, a close friend, Henry Charney, helped Levin land a sales job in his father's work glove factory, a fateful move which would set the stage for Levin's later career selling pottery. From the beginning, Levin had a knack for business, and envisioned a better life.

"He was always thinking about tomorrow," Jeanette elaborated. "During the Depression, Al would just toss away his coins; and when I started saving them in a glass jar, he'd say, 'I'm not interested in chasing nickels and pennies, just dollars!'" Over the next five years, Levin made steady progress towards bettering their lives; then suddenly, the attack on Pearl Harbor cast everyone's future into doubt.

Treasure Craft began in a single car garage in Gardena, California, 1947.

Bashful, the ancestor of five generations of Treasure Craft figurines. Circa 1949, 5" x 6", $24-28.

"Al was going to be drafted into the Army, so he decided the day before to enlist in the Navy instead," explained Jeanette. Sent from Great Lakes Training Center to the Pacific theater, he embarked on the aircraft carrier USS *Monterey* from Los Angeles' San Pedro Harbor. Serving as a medical corpsman, he suffered the hardships of war and separation from home faced by all brave sailors, yet developed a deep love of the Pacific.

"When he was released by the Navy, their policy was to return them where they enlisted, which meant he'd be discharged at Great Lakes," she adds. Levin was clearly impressed by the bustle, opportunity, and kind weather Southern California offered; he wired her to take the train from the frozen Midwest immediately.

"He had to say he had a job in California to avoid being sent back to Chicago," Jeanette continued. "I had to bring him a suit so he'd have civilian dress for interviews." He took a series of jobber positions, first supplying countertop snack racks to restaurants, then selling Gregorian Copper.

Levin was a hard worker and a good salesman. The couple saved a thousand dollars, using it as a down payment to buy a house in Gardena on the G.I. Bill. They moved in with baby daughter Jolene in December 1945.

"He sold a line of copper horse figures with detachable saddles, and he started taking it to gift stores. They sold okay, but the store owners kept mentioning that customers wanted pottery novelties that were in short supply." War material restrictions were just being lifted, and with the Axis in ruins, Germany and Japan were no longer players in ceramic production.

A Pottery Is Born

Levin asked questions and listened well, concluding that a line of ceramic mugs labeled "Mom", "Dad", and the like would sell. Home-based pottery firms were sprouting up all over California in response to demand, and he decided to have ceramic novelties made to order. In the kitchen of the Gardena house, he declared, "I'll make people little treasures … treasured crafts!" With a little tweaking, the newborn pottery was christened.

But contract production proved more difficult than it seemed. "Every time he'd place an order, these little home-based pottery businesses couldn't keep up with it," Jeanette opined. Levin finally found a reliable producer in the Laguna Beach pottery colony.

This crude little fellow is a very early brown elfin creature with the scarce Gardena ink stamp, 1947-1948 only, 5.5", $24-28.

Cope was the name of the pottery, its principals a young couple of the same name. Jeanette still pictured them vividly. "The husband was a towering red-headed man, at least six-foot-six", recalled the diminutive Mrs. Levin. "They lived in Laguna because

Alfred Levin on shore leave with wife Jeanette during World War II.

she loved making pottery and he loved swimming. They lived right in their studio; after a day's work, they'd clean off the workbench and lay a sleeping mat over it. Al would take them sketches, and they'd make models of things."

So in early 1947, the first of the Laguna-made pieces arrived to fill existing orders, and the Levin family car was evicted from the garage of the Gardena house, which became Treasure Craft's shipping and sales office. Jeanette, soon to give birth to son Bruce, became de facto shipping manager. "I had to drive to all the grocers and tell them that we were moving so I could get enough empty boxes," she laughed.

Along with mugs, *Naughty Gnomes* were among the first of the early lines. Though possessed of a certain crudeness, these elfin creatures, with their pointed ears and exaggerated, sculpted facial features, proved seminal to a 30-year run of "spritely" figurines. While clothing was glazed in appropriate colors, faces and hands were covered in Mrs. Stewart's Bluing ® so as to remain unglazed bisque. Eyes, lips, and facial details were hand-painted. Production ran high enough that many items were left unmarked, but a few bore the firm's first mark, a Treasure-Craft © Gardena, Calif. ink stamp.

Al Levin designed all of Treasure Craft's early ware, as illustrated in this sketchbook of his Sprite concepts.

Standing Elf and Sleigh, c. 1950, 5" and 4.5" x 8.5", respectively, $16-20/ea.

16   In the Beginning...

Novelty Salt-&-Peppers

A self-taught artist, Levin began to fill sketchbooks with elaborate designs and new ideas, evidencing a natural artistic talent that persisted the rest of his life. "He couldn't just sit and do nothing. He'd sit with the family while we enjoyed the radio or TV, making notes and drawing endlessly," Jeanette articulated. "He took inspiration from everything he saw."

He proved to have whimsical flair, quickly creating a line of novelty salt-and-pepper sets that paired not identically, but thematically...a chimp under a palm tree, a wrestler throwing his opponent, a slice of pie under a scoop of ice cream, a golf ball on a tee.

The semi-annual Los Angeles Gift Show proved a watershed for the fledgling firm; quality had improved with production increases, and the clever designs found ready orders in the post-war seller's market. Free-spirited and informal, the California lifestyle held sway in postwar America, and Treasure Craft wares were emblematic of it. Treasure Craft soon joined the California Art Potters Association, which capitalized on America's new obsession with the west.

"He had a natural design flair, but he was first and foremost a true businessman," explained Levin's son Bruce, who later worked alongside his father. "He liked to take a concept and see how far he could expand it." This trait resulted in a proliferation of shaker sets that began to tax the capacity of the single studio pottery in Laguna.

Elfin musicians, c. 1950, 4.5" to 5", $25-35/ea.

Rabbit and carrot shakers, c. 1950, 4.5" and 4.75". Originally sold for 49 cents; recent sales $18-22.

Phone and receiver shakers, c. 1950, 2", $15-18.

In the Beginning...

Lucky Sprites

But Levin saw opportunity, and pressed on with the development of a new line of medium sized, more refined elves known as *Lucky California Sprites*. Based on the Laguna gnomes, Sprites wore rich forest green glazes, but bore the unglazed bisque faces and hand-painted facial details of their larger predecessors. Molds were elaborately detailed, with defined collars, buckled belts, impressed ear details, and hand-painted eyes and lips.

Appealing to gift buyers and collectors, individual Sprites were given names, which were marked on matching printed gift boxes. A slip of paper printed with the lore of the Lucky California Sprites was slipped into each box:

> I am a Lucky California Sprite
> From 'way deep in the forest I have just come
> To find out how peoples' lives are run.
> I've found that there are troubles galore
> And so I'm glad I have brought my store.
> I'll bring you joy and I'll bring you cheer,
> I'll bring you luck throughout the year,
> I'm a Lucky California Sprite-
> and if you'd keep your luck just right-
> just rub my hands and forehead too, and
> I promise to save all my luck for you!

With Levin's packaging, Cope's Sprites qualified for a design patent in 1949. A country enjoying relief from the gritty war years sought frivolity and orders for the new line came fast. More production capacity was needed. A portion of a building next to a cleaning and dyeing plant in nearby South Gate was leased, and Levin began the transition from pottery agent to manufacturer.

"Al always had the big picture in front of him, and he was good at finding other people who could do the detail work," asserted Jeanette. "Even when he was still just contracting production, his associates nicknamed him 'Boss'." But expanding from a studio operation required equipment, and working knowledge of firing and kiln processes Levin did not possess.

Happy Sprite candy box, c. 1950, 5.5" x 7", $50-60.

Designer Turns Producer

Levin found his answer in Lee Shank, hired as Treasure Craft's first plant manager. A veteran of various small potteries in the L.A. basin, she helped assemble an able staff of mold casters, kiln operators, decorators, and finishers. From the beginning, about three-quarters of the workers were Hispanic, many from central Mexico. Most decorators were women.

Cope and Al Levin received a 1949 patent for their boxed elfin Sprites with paper legends enclosed. Snoopy the Sprite ledge hanger, box, lore, 1949, 4", $32-36.

Wee Wuns were half-sized elfin figures Treasure Craft added around 1950. *Wee Dee* on Trolley planter, $24-28.

In the Beginning. . .

The timing of the expansion proved fortunate. Sprites found a national audience, and Levin built a sales force that included the Edward Darvill organization and inside salesman Al Schulman. Cope's rights were purchased around 1950, and Treasure Craft expanded old and new lines for both of the year's major houseware shows. The miniature *Wee Wuns* line debuted, half-sized elfin creatures with names like Wee Dee and Wee Gee, clad in leafy costumes. Ink stamped marks changed to reflect the new location, while new paper labels adhered to the bottom of fully glazed pieces.

By 1951, Treasure Craft was offering over a hundred different pieces and operating a second, 10,000 square foot plant at 4427 Firestone Boulevard in South Gate. Inspired by the success of striated ware by Barbara Willis and others, the firm created *Scratch Ware*; though not a great seller, it opened a vast new tableware market to Treasure Craft. A line of brightly colored fruit wall pockets was added, and Sprites began to adorn leafy wall pockets, lazy susans, and sugar bowls alongside the traditional garden ware.

Treasure Craft grew to become a manufacturer in this South Gate plant in the early '50s.

Early items like this Hors d' Oeuvres line have seldom been identified as Treasure Craft by collectors. 4.5" to 8", $15-28/ea.

California Pottery Sweeps America

A major new force rocked the ceramics industry in 1951. Registered California Association, a giftware trade promotion group, opened a showroom at the Brack Shops. The association stole that summer's New York Gift Show, exhibiting California wares in suites near the main show site. Excitement over California style was at its zenith, and Treasure Craft was judged worthy of membership in the association. (Collectors have occasionally found early Treasure Craft pieces still wearing tiny round *Registered California* labels.)

"The nation looks to California to establish style trends," boasted Registered California's *Pictorial* in February 1952. Emblematic of those trends were Treasure Craft's new Stage Coach Sprites, a trellis vase and textured wall pocket, sharing space in the publication with figurines by Florence Ceramics, Brayton Laguna, and Hedi Schoop. Sent to giftware buyers across America, the gazette drew many requests for Treasure Craft's 1952 price sheet, which had grown to ten pages.

In just five short years, Treasure Craft had grown from a mom-and-pop contractor in a single-car garage to a nationally recognized pottery producer with five different lines. Treasure Craft's handful of small plants sprinkled through South Gate hummed with activity, and the Levins were able to move from the Gardena tract house to the fashionable Westwood area of Los Angeles. Treasure Craft seemed destined for glory; but these early successes masked a menacing new power the industry was about to face.

This 1952 Sprite ad sheet extolled Treasure Craft's presence in Registered California's permanent display at the Brack Shops in Los Angeles. Planters not shown elsewhere: 1907 Olds, $40-45; Fire Wagon, $45-50; Money Bag, $25-30.

Registered California helped introduce California pottery to the rest of America in 1951.

Sprite Stagecoach and Horse wall pocket set, c. 1950, 6" x 8" and 4" x 4". Stagecoach, $42-48; Horse, $15-18.

In the Beginning. . .

South Gate Salt & Peppers, 1947-1955

Pie A La Mode shakers, c. 1950, 1.75", $10-15.

Catalog photo of themed novelty shakers, c. 1950, $15-18/ea.

Drunk shaker in search of his Lamp Post, c. 1950, 4", $18-20 (set).

Mexican Hat Dance shakers, c. 1950, 3.25", $12-16.

Golf Ball and Tee shakers, c. 1950, 3.25", $12-16.

Football and Megaphone shakers, c. 1950, 3.5", $12-16.

In the Beginning... 21

Artist and Palette shakers, c. 1950, 2.5", $15-18.

Monkey and Banana shakers, c. 1950, 1.25", $15-18.

Horned Toad and Cactus shakers, 3", $12-16.

Monkey and Palm Tree shakers, c. 1950, 3.75", $18-20.

Lunch Pail and Thermos shakers, c. 1950, 3.25", $10-15.
Burger and Pop shakers, c. 1950, 3", $18-20.

Wrestlers shakers, c. 1950, 4.5", $18-24.

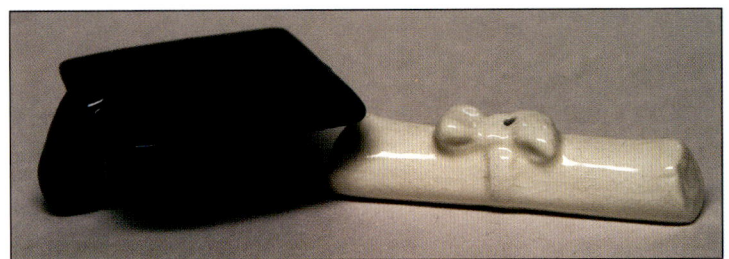

Diploma and Cap shakers, c. 1950, .75", $12-16.

Lazy Mexican and Wife shakers from the politically incorrect '50s, 4.25", $18-20.

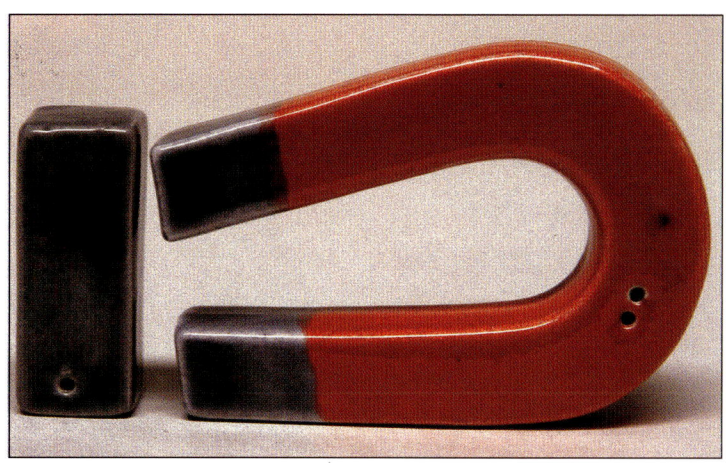

Magnet and Bar shakers, c. 1950, 2", $10-15.

Hammer and Anvil shakers, c. 1950, 2", $12-15.

Truck and Tanker shakers, c. 1952, 2", $18-20. Car and Trailer shakers, c. 1952, 1.75", $18-20.

Nut and Bolt shakers, c. 1950, .75", $12-15.
Life Ring shakers, 3", $15-18.

Barn and Silo shakers, c. 1950, 2.25", $12-15. Desk and Books shakers, c. 1950, 1.75", $10-15.

In the Beginning. . .

Lighthouse and Tender shakers, c. 1950, 3.5", $15-20.

Pirate and Chest shakers, c. 1950, 1.75", $15-18. Flat Tire and Pump shakers, c. 1950, 2.25", $15-18.

Outhouse and Catalogue shakers, c. 1950, 3.5", $10-15.

Indian in Canoe shakers, c. 1950, 2.5", $20-25. Covered Wagon and Oxen, c. 1950, 2.25", $12-15.

Briefcase and Hat shakers, c. 1950, 1.75", $12-15.

Cigarettes and Matches shakers, c. 1950, 3.5", $18-24.

Mail Box and Letter shakers, c. 1950, 3.75", $16-20.

24   In the Beginning. . .

Boxing Gloves and Bag shakers, c. 1950, 2.75", $12-15.

Baseball and Mitt shakers, c. 1950, 1.75", $12-15.

Santa and Toys shakers, c. 1952, 2.75", $15-20.

Penguin and Igloo shakers, c. 1950, 2.5", $10-15.

Scrub Brush and Bucket shakers, c. 1950, 2.25", $10-15.

Boots and Creel shakers, c. 1950, 3.5", $12-15.

Birthday Cake and Package shakers, c. 1950, 1.5", $15-20.

In the Beginning... 25

Bread and Butter shakers, c. 1950, 2", $12-15.

Banana Split shakers, c. 1950, 1.25", $16-20.

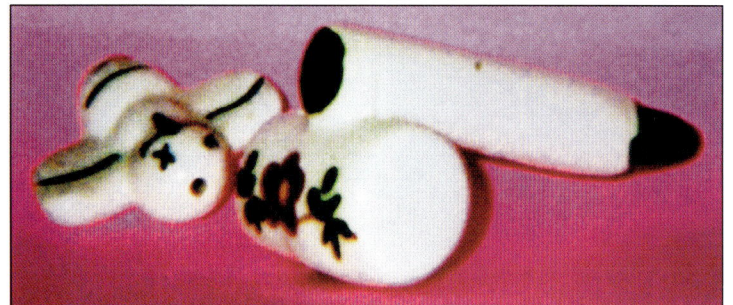
Fly and Sprayer shakers, c. 1950, .75", $14-18.

Lucky California Sprites, 1949-1956

Chartreuse was Treasure Craft's first new Sprite color, shown on this c. 1950 *Helpful* fence planter, 5.5" x 6.25", $30-35.

Lucky Sprite on leaf wall pocket, c. 1950, 7.75" x 7", $48-55.

This Sprite watering can still bears its Registered California label, c. 1952, 4.25", $24-28.

Dreamy Sprite on log planters, c. 1950, 3" x 7.5". (Green tips on Chartreuse came later.) $20-24/ea.

Sprite on nest planter, c. 1950, 5.75", $32-35.

Sprite rock wall bench planter, c. 1950, 4" x 7.5", $22-25.

Sprite lore on foil label and box with ink stamped name, 1949. Presence adds $10-15, depending on piece.

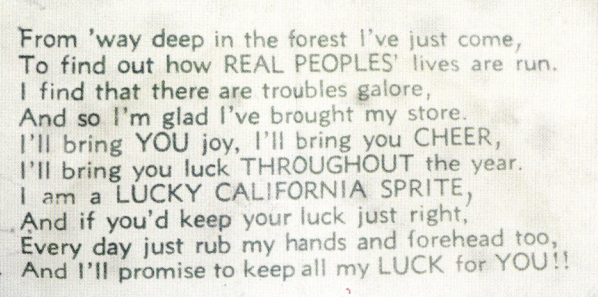

In the Beginning. . .

Sprite on Stump cigarette box, c. 1950, 4.25", $25-30.

Groovy, slotted shelf sitter, c. 1950, 3", $15-18.

Sprite on Boot planter, c. 1950, 4.5", $15-18.

Sprite kneeling at stump bud vase, c. 1950, 5.75", $18-20.

Hopeful, c. 1950, 3", $14-16.

28   In the Beginning. . .

Sprite cigarette box, tray (originally came with two), c. 1950, 5.5" x 6.25" (trays, 3.5"), $40-45/set.

Cheerful Sprite at wishing well wall pocket, c. 1950, 5", $25-28.

Sprite Woodsman planter, c. 1950, 4.25", $22-25.

Sprite on barrel wall pocket (replete with period plastic ivy), c. 1950, 5", $28-32.

In the Beginning. . . 29

Wee Wuns, 1950-1956

Wee Wun Boat planter featuring *Wee Gee*, c. 1950, 4.25" x 6", $25-29.

Wee Breeze on tree swing, c. 1950, 3.75", $24-28.

Wee Wun Pump planter, c. 1950, 4" x 7.75", $24-28.

Wee Ho praying at wishing well planter, c. 1950, 3.25", $15-19.

Shoe planter, the biggest seller of the line, c. 1950, 3.75", $12-15.

Wee Wun on log, c. 1950, 2.75" x 6", $18-20.

30   In the Beginning. . .

House planter, c. 1950, 4", $25-29 (aqua, $38-42).

Two different styles of trunk bud vases, c. 1950, 4", $12-15/ea. Wee Wun Trellis vase, c. 1950, $24-27.

Foil labels for tourist sites were a new idea when this Stump planter was made around 1950, 3.5", $15-18.

Wee Lu, c. 1950, 3", $15-17.

In the Beginning... 31

Pixies, early 1950s

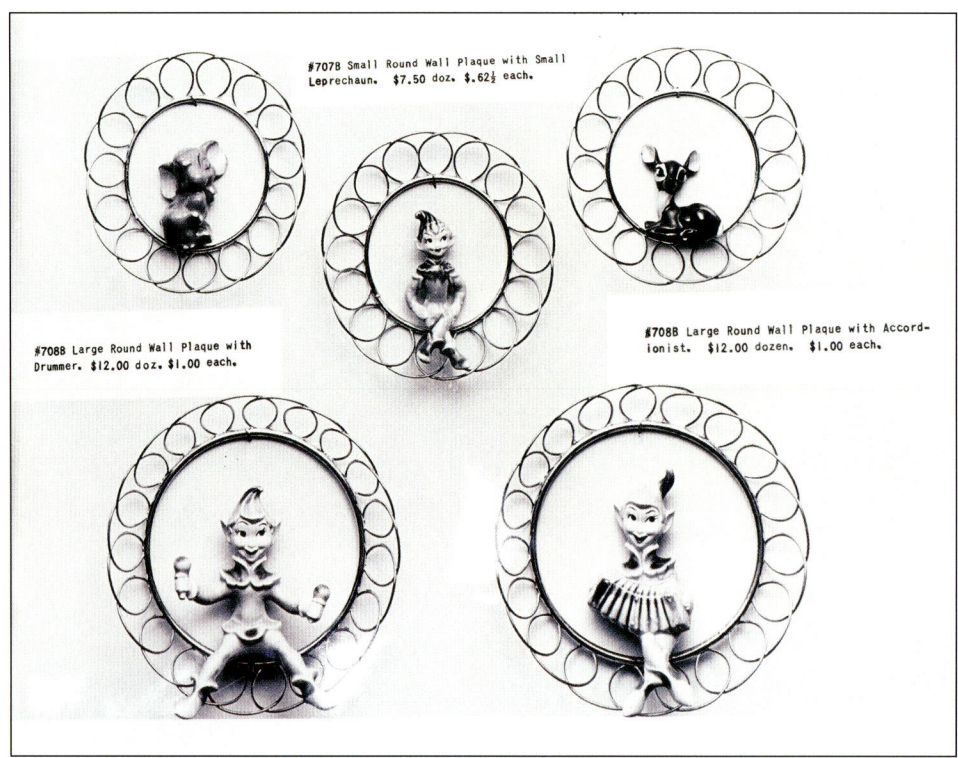

Treasure Craft's short-lived Pixies line shown with other airbrushed figures, c. 1955.

Pixie piano planter, c. 1955, 4.25". (Note different coloring and lack of ear impressions compared to Sprites.) $30-35.

More Pixie musicians, c. 1955.

32   In the Beginning. . .

Wall Pockets, early 1950s

Fruit wall pockets, c. 1950. (Metal surrounds were an extra embellishment.) Red apple in wire, 9.5", $35-39. Strawberry, 6.25", $32-35. Green Apple, 6.25", $20-24.

Bananas wall pocket in surround, South Gate script mark in-mold, c. 1950, 8.75", $35-39.

Pear wall pocket lamp, c. 1953, 13". (It's unknown whether Treasure Craft bought lamp parts or sold the pockets to a lamp maker.) $40-45.

In the Beginning. . .

Transition to Compton: 1955-1959

California pottery's splash at the 1951 New York Gift Show proved to be the peak of the industry. That same year, an ominous new force faced American potteries.

As an extension of the Marshall Plan, American funds went to help rebuild the German and Japanese ceramics industries, whose absence had allowed the California potters to prosper. A huge tariff reduction on ceramic imports led to a flood of cheap Japanese pottery, particularly small figurines.

Yet somehow, Treasure Craft continued to grow. Gift buyers found extra value in the Sprite's gift boxes and lore tags, and fun new thematic shakers like the surfer and surfboard or the dog with master's slipper held sway over matched pairs from overseas. Novel ideas kept the line growing, and gold leaf was introduced as an option on a new sleigh planter and rooster cigarette set. For the holidays, a small line of red clad Sprites were joined by a few similarly decorated *Santa* figures.

It helped that Treasure Craft's earthenware was light to ship when compared with Ohio pottery. Ordered from Westwood Ceramics, the talc-rich clays (with ingredients from as far as Tennessee and Kentucky) were blended at the new Compton plants. New plants and equipment kept production inexpensive, so even large pieces remained sufficiently price competitive.

Sprite with Cart, red, c. 1952, 5" x 7", $25-30.

Marked *Occupied Japan* by law, these early imports were often of dubious quality-but the price was right. Japanese pixies wholesaled for as little as 7 cents apiece, while Treasure Craft Sprites and other California elves cost 30 to 50 cents. America's five-and-dime stores readily substituted Japanese wares, and small California potteries began to fail in droves.

Lazy Sprites, 4.25". Maroon, c. 1953, $20-24.
Forest, c. 1950, $12-15.

Granny in Rocker shakers, c. 1950, 4", $14-18.

New lines moved with popular 1950s themes, like the wagon wheel hors-d'-oeuvres tray and the pistol-and-holster salt and pepper. The older Sprite line wore trendy new colors like aqua and pink, maroon and tan, white and chartreuse. A scroll-shaped, red on gold foil label with a treasure chest declared them Treasure-Craft Originals, a flourish of quality.

Wagon Wheel hors d' oeuvres, c. 1953, 7", $24-28.

Wood Stain

The mid-'50s colors and some interesting glazes with gold speckling or swirling kept the ware up to date, but Levin saw a need for a new style of hand decoration that would transcend color fads and Japanese copies. Treasure Craft began experimenting with the newly popular decorating technique of using wood stain on ceramic bisque. Instead of the usual solid green, a bare bisque tree trunk was hand rubbed with a ruddy brown wood stain, giving naturalistic contrast to the aqua Sprite perched at its base.

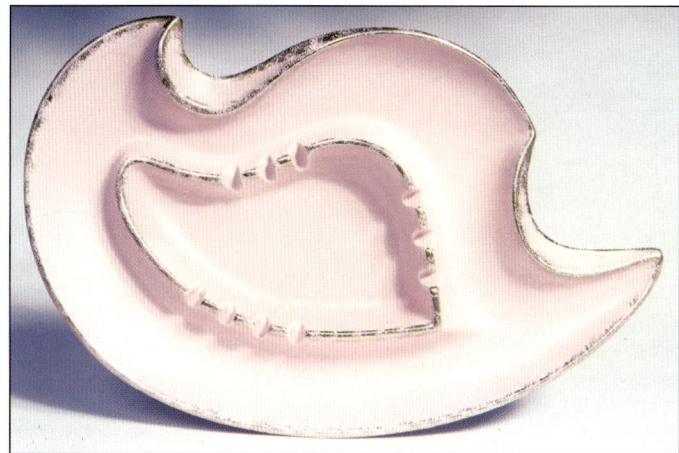

Scroll ashtray, #33, pink, 1957 only, 12.5", $16-20.

Developed by the UCLA and USC ceramics schools in the late 1930s, this technique was commercially pioneered by Barbara Willis, first used to highlight her striated vases in the early '40s. By the time of Treasure Craft's experiment, Brayton Laguna designer Carol Safholm was employing a dark rubbed stain to contrast with painted highlights, debuting a dramatic line of African dancers in 1952.

Wood staining offered an inexpensive alternative to the meticulous hand detailing the Sprite faces required, and Levin and plant manager Lee Shank set about perfecting the technique. *Wood Stain* or *Walnut* were the monikers applied to the brown rubbed finish, formulated to match the warm, natural wood tones of '50s modern cabinetry. It took several attempts for Treasure Craft and their partners at Elixir to concoct a wood stain that would gradate realistically and adhere to clay.

The perfection of wood stain offered another important advantage. Finished with a lacquer coat, it didn't need a second firing, saving time, energy, and the large numbers of pieces typically lost in the firing process.

Experimental aqua Sprite on ruddy wood stained trunk, c. 1952, 4.25", $35-40.

Tony Guerrero was hired as Treasure Craft's first in-house art director. Over the next decade, he profoundly changed the firm's designs to suit the new stain. Guerrero's sculptural skill was first evidenced in a new line of TV lamps that featured a graceful leaping gazelle, double horse heads with flowing mane, and a stylish pair of drama masks.

White trim glazes were painted onto raw greenware and fired before the rubbed finish was added. Formulated to shrink at a different rate than the clay in firing, the white would attractively crackle. Crisp details gave the lamps a luxurious appearance, opening a new, premium market to Treasure Craft.

"No one had seen pottery designed to exactly match furniture tones that way," explained Jeanette Levin of wood stain's inaugural success. While Brayton had rubbed an even chocolate color over striated surfaces to suggest wood, Guerrero chose instead to sculpt detailed wood grain into his original models. The warm brown stain pooled more darkly in the more deeply carved areas, suggesting the dark and light variations inherent in natural materials. Treasure Craft's new color could realistically match wood, brown skin or hair.

Comedy and Tragedy mask lamp, Guerrero, South Gate, scarce, c. 1955, 8.5", $100-125.

Compton and the Fire

Stores selling home decor clamored for more accent pieces to match their '50s Scandinavian Modern furniture, and Treasure Craft again faced the need to expand. Levin began searching for a site to augment his several small South Gate operations, first occupying a building at the corner of Alameda and Carlin in Compton.

Levin sought to consolidate operations in Compton, and bought a larger plant at 2320 N. Alameda in 1955. "It was a greasy old industrial plant, and it took three months just to clean," Jeanette reflected. Even then, Compton was tough and gritty; when his father first showed the plant to eight-year-old Bruce, they had to cautiously step around a craps game in progress to get to the front door.

The new plant was scarcely operational when devastation struck. An overnight kiln explosion burned the new factory to ash. Pottery plants were considered high risk, and insurance had proven unobtainable. All seemed lost.

Gazelle television lamp, sculpted by art director Tony Guerrero, South Gate foil label, c. 1955, 11", $85-95.

Double horse head lamp, Guerrero, South Gate, c. 1955, 9", $55-65.

Treasure Craft's largest plant in Compton burned in a devastating 1955 fire, but loyal employees helped the firm rebuild a modern new facility on the same site.

But Levin's loyal employees stood by him. Without production, there was no money to pay them, yet they helped sift through the ashes to recover any molds or equipment they could. In later years, Levin cited in particular the efforts of Ray Hunt, a volunteer fireman who worked at the plant, and Johnny Dickson, Levin's maintenance supervisor. "Dad often said it was Johnny Dickson who held the plant together," Bruce Levin recounted.

Fortunately, the South Gate plants were spared destruction, and resumed production of the salvaged lines. A larger plant was rebuilt on the fire site, and the task of developing wood stain wares resumed.

Aqua bowl, one of the last South Gate colors, c. 1955, 6", $6-8.

Guerrero's Dancers

Xavier Cugat, Desi Arnaz, and other musicians created a fever for Caribbean music and dance in the mid-'50s. Drawing on his Hispanic heritage and Levin's design suggestions, Guerrero advanced a series of sinuous figurines performing different styles of Latin dance.

"Tony was masterful at designing pieces with fluid motion," marveled Bruce Levin about Guerrero's work. Treasure Craft dancers were captured mid-step, the men boasting powerful physiques, the women curvaceous and well proportioned. His thoughtful designs achieved this using two-piece molds and eliminating as many casting steps as possible, an important consideration in the increasingly cutthroat pottery business.

Flamenco Dancer and Conga Drummer, Guerrero, c. 1955, 11.5" man and 10.5" woman. No marks, $100-125/pair.

Unlike other California figurines, Guerrero modeled eyes and facial details to be deliberately abstract, not intended to be hand-detailed. Instead, sculpted musculature and detailed clothing were emphasized. White crackle glazes set off the dancers' costumes, from the ruffled skirt and conga drum of the *Flamenco Dancers* to the *Adagio* couple's fluttering scarves. Wood stain was rubbed over entire pieces, highlighting the crackling and darkening the skin and hair.

The figurines were an artistic success, elevating Treasure Craft's giftware reputation beyond the aging Sprite and shaker lines, which were beginning to be phased out of production. But at the then lofty sum of ten dollars per pair, Levin knew sales of the figurines would be limited. Wood stain would have to reach the broader tableware market to support the expanded company.

Adagio Dancers, Guerrero, scarce, c. 1955, 10" man and 5.5" x 9.5" woman. No marks, $125-150/pair.

Señor and Señorita, Guerrero, c. 1957, 12" man and 10.5" woman. No marks, $95-110/pair.

In the meantime, existing solid color lines were converted to wood stain. Novelty ashtrays styled in 1956 included a gaping fish and a *Ubangi* maiden; offered from South Gate in red, aqua, white, and black, they soon were paralleled in brown at the Compton plant.

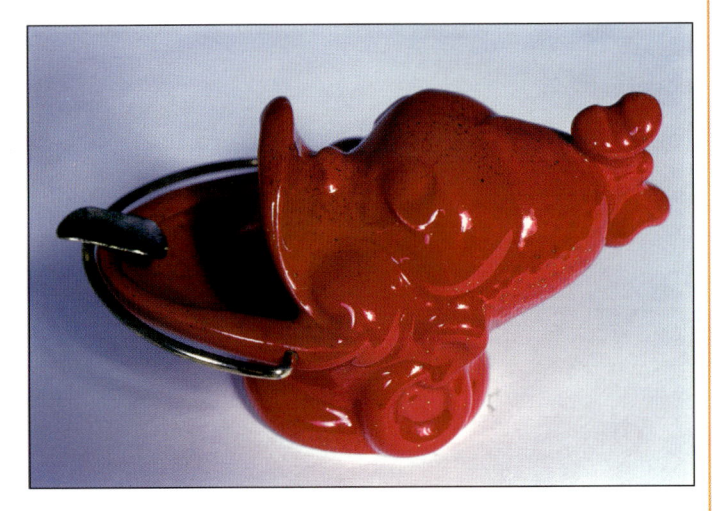

Ubangi ashtray, red, South Gate ink stamp, 1956 only, 3.5" x 6.5", $28-32.

Western Styles

But the real dilemma was how to transform wood tone finishes into appealing lines of kitchenware. Levin was inspired to merge 1950s western mania with his new earth tones in a new line of barrel-shaped serving pieces.

Barrel Line was a big gamble for Treasure Craft. Unlike prior lines, which evolved in stages, Levin understood he had to offer a complete line of canisters, butter and cheese dishes, and other serving pieces if he was to defy America's mid-'50s obsession with pastels and lurid reds.

Barrel Line canisters with copper strips were a hit when introduced late in 1955. Flour (1950s version, ceramic finial), 8.5", $13-16. Tea and Coffee (1970s wood finials), 7.5", $12-14/ea.

The woodsy new service debuted in November 1955, just in time for the holidays-and just ahead of the 1956 gift show season. A quarter page section in that month's *Giftwares* magazine proclaimed that the eleven-piece set of pottery barrels had "the rich appearance of fine hand-finished natural wood...trimmed with copper". Prices were held low, the large cookie jar retailing for $5.10, the spice jars just $2.50 each.

Eleven pieces of Barrel sold in the introductory line. Not shown elsewhere: Beer mug, 4.25", $9-12; Coffee cups, $5-6; shakers, $8-12 (range size $10-15); cream and sugar, $6-8/ea.; chip and suspended dips, 10.5", $20-25.

38   Transition to Compton: 1955-1959

Barrel was an instant hit! Two copper bands made the wood stained kitchenware resemble authentic antique oaken barrels, a radical departure from the offerings of other pottery firms. While Treasure Craft's stylish figurines attracted modern decorators, Barrel found favor with fans of the decade's other major decorating trend towards rustic and neo-colonial design.

First offered with the experimental ruddy tint, Barrel's wood stain soon became warm and chocolaty, a neutral tone that could mix with any color, or stand alone. Harmonious with many kitchens, Barrel would expand to comprise dozens of pieces, becoming a Treasure Craft mainstay over an incredible twenty year run.

The obvious appeal of western styles led Guerrero and Levin to add new figurines. The most recognized appeared in 1958, a charging bull faced by a matador in an intricately detailed coat.

The set attracted the attention of Sperry and Hutchinson, whose Green Stamp Redemption Centers offered premiums to grocery patrons who received S&H stamps with purchases. Inclusion in the *S&H Giftbook* opened a new world of customers to Treasure Craft, and S&H soon became their largest account.

A rearing bull would be added, and its success spawned other animal figurines. A pair of *Stallions* were coupled with a striking *Cowboy* figure, and a scarcely seen elephant joined a new Chinese line, whose *Buddha*, busts, *Emperor and Empress* were offered in gold leaf as well as Wood Stain.

Circa 1957 Barrel add-ons. Pitchers: milk, 1 qt., $15-18; juice, 1.5 qt., $18-20; water, 2 qt., $20-24.

Matador and side-facing bull, Guerrero, c. 1958, 8.5" and 6.25" x 10". No marks, $45-50.

Transition to Compton: 1955-1959

Wire Ware

The metal and wire bands that gave Barrel its pizzazz presented a new manufacturing challenge. Facing uneven quality and the difficulty of fitting the wire to the pieces, Levin opted to hire skilled metalworkers and install metal fabricating machinery at the Compton plant.

The endless possibilities of wire bending led to an entirely new line, as existing planters were fitted to wall hanging wire holders in rococo and modernistic styles. A corollary line called *Hacienda Ware* was devoted almost entirely to the metalworkers' art, with only minor ceramic accessories added.

Functional wire gift ware followed. Within a few years, pottery butterflies and hens were outfitted as letter holders, while ashtrays rode in cat or sailboat shaped wire caddies. Though wire ware eventually became passé, some pieces stayed in the line until the 1970s.

Wire work was done in-house at Treasure Craft in the 1950s and '60s, $12-24/ea.

A Major California Pottery Arrives

As the 1950s closed, Al Levin's gamble was paying off handsomely, even as the American pottery industry struggled.

Levin's vision presaged the shift to earth tones that would sweep the country in the 1960s and '70s, and art director Guerrero translated that vision into a plethora of new designs. Chief among them was a second successful tableware pattern, *Fruitwood Line*, its lightly stained fruit designs greatly contrasting against darker, bark textured backgrounds. The striking visual impact of this sculpting technique taught a lesson Treasure Craft would utilize throughout its history.

In 1959, Treasure Craft of Hawaii formed. Compton redesigned old lines for the new venture, and Guerrero started sculpting new hula dancer figurines. Intended to simply produce tourist wares for inter-island distribution, the Maui facility's design needs would take the firm in an exciting new direction, convergent with the emerging beach culture of the early '60s.

From a Gardena garage had emerged a major player in the California pottery industry.

Tony Guerrero Figurines of the 1950s

Matador with optional rearing bull, 1958. Bull: 9.5" x 11", $45-55.

Matador with charging bull, the leading sellers of the California wood stain figurines (originally sold separately or as set). Matador: Treasure Craft 19©58 impressed mark, 13", $24-28. Bull: 7" x 14.5". No marks, $40-50.

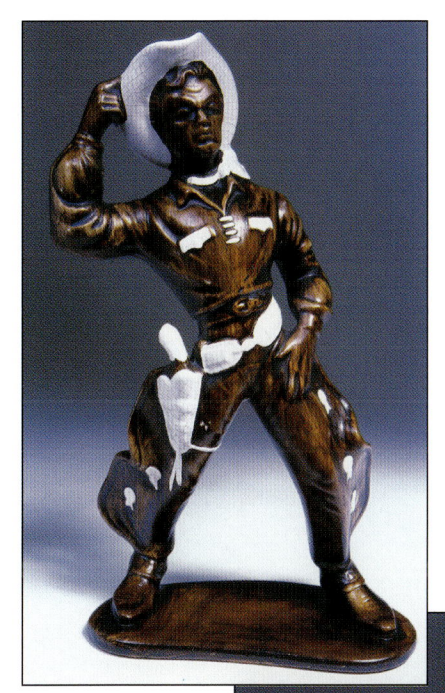

Cowboy, c. 1958, 11.5". No marks, $60-70.

Old West Figures

Stallions, c. 1958, 7" and 9.25". No marks, $30-35 and $40-50.

Rear view of '50s cowboy shows attention to detail and motion.

Troubador Mice

Mouse Troubadours, c. 1958, 10" with sombreros, 9" with straw hats. Hawaii or Compton marks on rear of bases, $40-50/ea.

Stallion, rearing, c. 1958, 10.25" x 11". No marks, $40-50.

Transition to Compton: 1955-1959 41

Chinese Busts

Chinese Busts, c. 1959, 13". No marks, $75-85/set.

Harem Guard

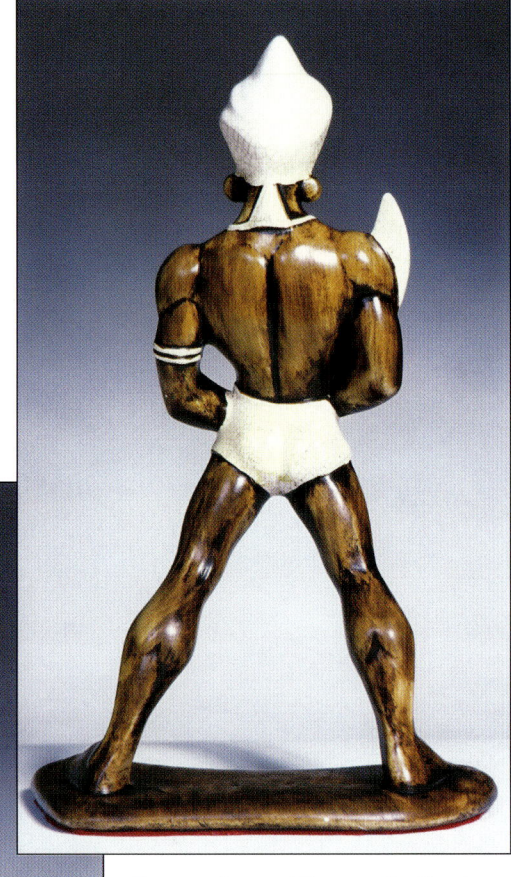

Guerrero's guard figure embodies the sculptor's focus on physique. (Matching harem dancer presumed, but unknown to author.)

Harem guard, scarce, c. 1958, 12". No marks, $100-120.

42 Transition to Compton: 1955-1959

360-Degree Design

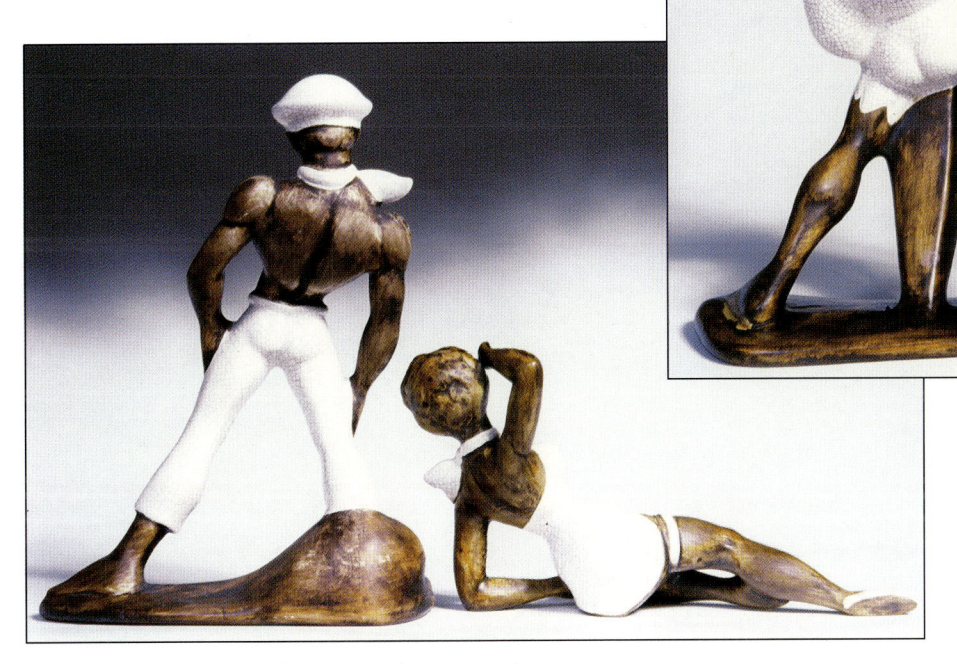

Rear detail of dancing couples suggested motion without requiring extra castings and applications of parts.

Rear view of Spanish Dancers.

Transition to Compton: 1955-1959 43

Gold Leaf

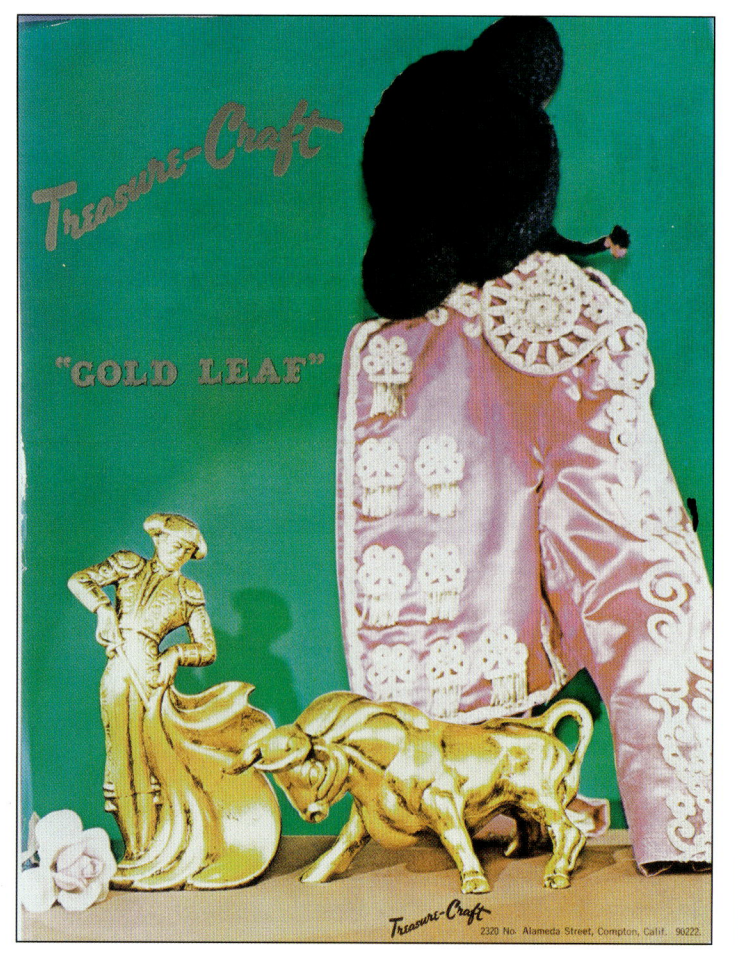

Gold Leaf sales sheet, c. 1960.

Gold Leaf catalogue, late 1950s. Values on the known items have tended to run 20-30% above their wood stained counterparts.

Gold Leaf Chinese Line figures, c. 1960. Not enough of these scarcities have yet reached the market to establish current prices.

44   Transition to Compton: 1955-1959

Last South Gate Lines, ca. 1957

Pink and aqua glazes were swirled with gold in experiments near the end of South Gate production, c. 1956, 4", $22-25.

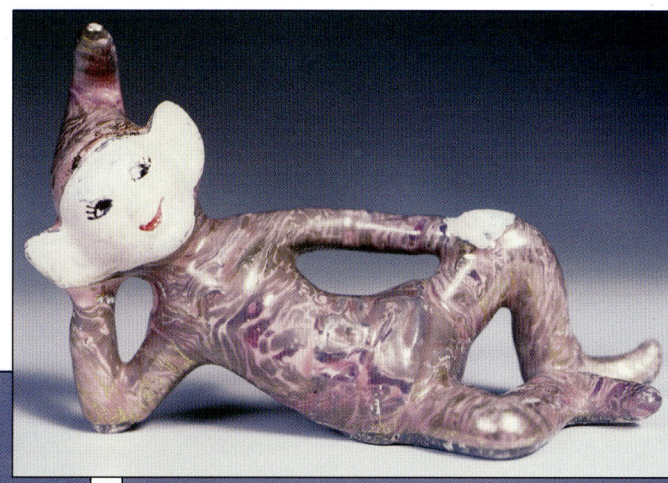

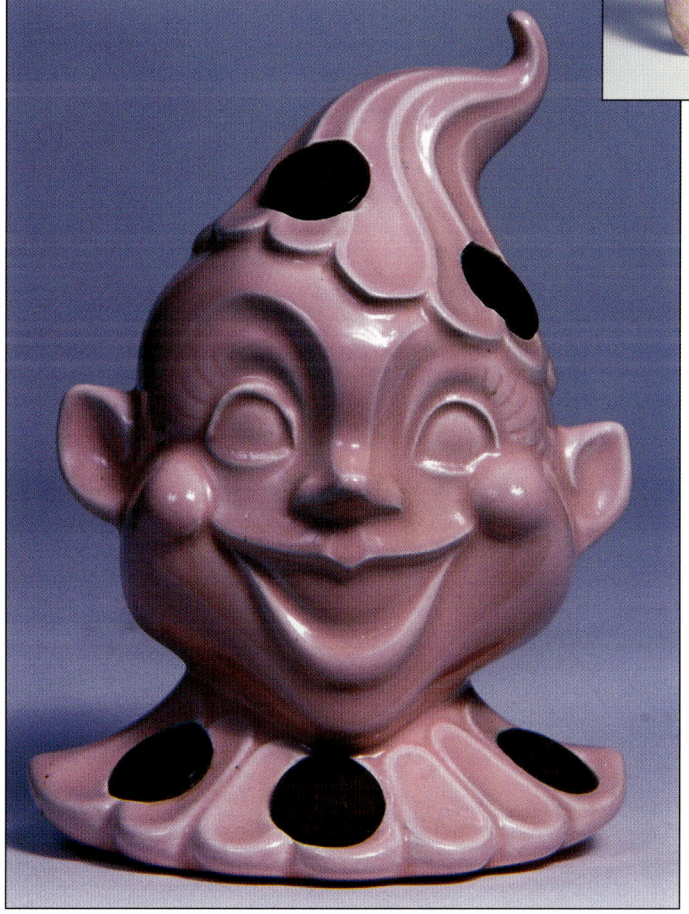

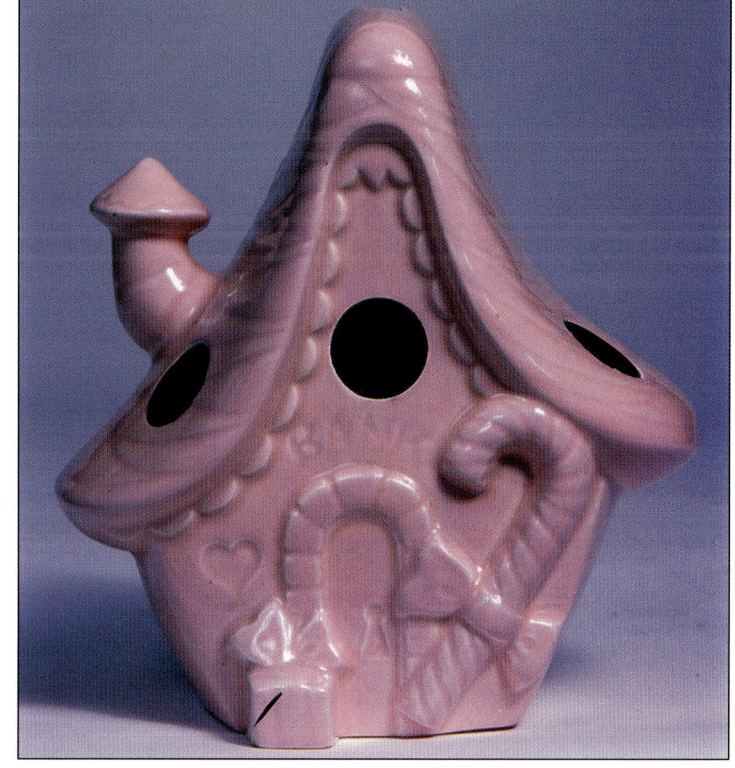

House bank with applied pennies, 1957, 5.25", $40-50.

Leprechaun bank with applied, pennies, 1957, 5.5", $40-50.

Gold speckling was another late South Gate color effect, c. 1956, 3.25", $24-28.

Transition to Compton: 1955-1959 45

Tableware

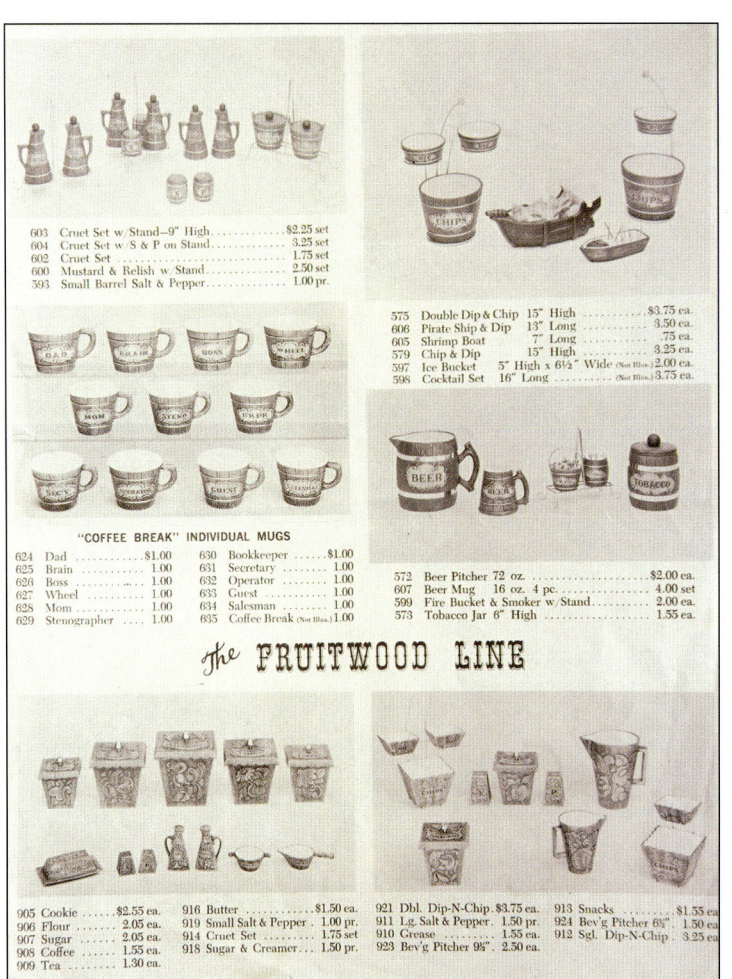

Barrel Line not shown elsewhere:
    Beer pitcher, $22-25.
    Chip and dip set, ship, $25-30.
    Condiment pots, $9-12/ea.
    Cruets, $18-20/pr.
    Humidor, $24-28.
    Smoking set in wire holder, $14-18.

Fruitwood Line:
    Butter/lid, $10-12.
    Canister, lg., $10-14.
    Canister, sm., $9-12.
    Canister, snack, $9-12.
    Cookie jar, $12-18.
    Cruets, $14-18/pr.
    Chip and dip, $12-15.
    Chip and dips, $15-20.
    Creamer, stick, $6-8.
    Grease jar, $12-15.
    Pitcher, milk, $12-15.
    Pitcher, water, $15-18.
    Shakers, table, $5-7.
    Shakers, range, $6-8.
    Sugar, open, $5-7.

Barrel Shrimp Boat with dip insert, c. 1957, 4.5", $12-15.

By 1957, Barrel Line grew to a complete set of kitchen and table accessories.

46   Transition to Compton: 1955-1959

Double chip and dip in early ruddy stain, c. 1955, 13.5", $20-25.

Colonial embossed scene cup, 1958, 4", $6-8.

Vases and Planters

Harp planter, derived from Pixie Musicians line, 1958, 6.5", $10-13.

Crackle leaf bud vase, c. 1957, 8", $20-24.

Spinning Wheel planter, 1958, 7", $12-15.

Transition to Compton: 1955-1959 47

New Trays, 1959

Pod leaf two-section dish (progenitor of 1960s serving ware), #375, 14.75", $14-18.

Rooster hors d' oeuvres in four-section fruit border tray, c. 1959, 5.25" x 13.5", $18-22/set.

Novelty Ashtrays

Novelty ashtray ad slick, c. 1960. Tiki head, 3.5", $20-22. Ubangi, 4", $18-20. Elephant, 3.5", $14-18. Others: $10-15/ea.

Within a few years, the four-section tray was adorned by many different colored glazes and hors d' oeuvres holders like the Menehune Pineapple, $24-28/set.

Treasure Craft of Hawaii: 1959-1984

Luscious valleys, mountain waterfalls, volcanoes, and sandy beaches swarmed by today's tourists belie conditions on Maui as Hawaiian statehood approached in 1959.

Only thirteen of Maui High School's 166 seniors planned to remain on their beautiful island after graduation that year, according to the *Maui News*. Most tourists had only heard of Waikiki, and the Valley Isle's few hotel rooms sat largely vacant. The sugar industry, backbone of Maui's plantation economy, had mechanized and idled many workers.

Replacing the Sugar Plantations

By 1959, Maui had lost a quarter of its pre-war population. Plantation owners Alexander & Baldwin sought new industry to fill its vacant sugar factories, seeking to turn the war port of Kahului into a vigorous new town. A business *hui (council)* formed to seek mainland firms to invest, and A&B's Frank Churchill, realtor Earling P. Wick, Doc Lyons of Maui Electric, and others called on the California pottery industry in 1958. Dale C. Kennedy of L.A. Potteries and Treasure Craft's Alfred Levin agreed to come see what Maui offered.

For Levin, the visit presented more than the opportunity to make and sell pottery in Hawaii. He'd fallen in love with the islands during his time in the Navy during World War II, and shared America's fascination with its Polynesian territory. Together with Kennedy and Wick, he surprised the industry by leasing an old A&B power plant at 590 Haleakala Highway, a few blocks from Kahului Harbor.

The result was the first full-scale pottery operation in the islands since the Hawaiian Potters Guild of the 1930s. Despite the partnership with L.A. Potteries, the designs and production processes were unmistakably Treasure Craft's, as was the name of the joint venture. Together with Tony Guerrero, art director at Treasure Craft's mainland plant in Compton, Levin created a new line of designs derived from Hawaiian cultural icons.

Tony Guerrero sculpted the Hula Girl, Drummer Boy, and Uli Uli Boy for the new Hawaiian plant, 1959, 10.5"-11.5". Drummer, $60-70. Others, $50-60.

Under the shadow of Haleakala, the port of Kahului offered easy inter-island and mainland shipping.

Now a surfboard factory, this old Maui sugar plant served as Treasure Craft's Hawaiian home for a quarter-century.

Treasure Craft founder Al Levin (right) on Maui with friend Bob Vossler, c. 1959.

Hawaiian Icons by Guerrero

Known to locals as *ki'i* and tourists as *tiki gods*, *akua ki'i la'au* were wood sculptures the ancient Hawaiians carved to idolize island deities. Western intrigue with them began when a Ku war god image arrived in Boston in 1825, but their abolishment by King Kamehameha II rendered them largely unknown until tourists rediscovered them decades later.

Guerrero's interpretation of Ku bore the idol's threatening, toothy grimace and flared nostrils in exacting detail. Brushed with Treasure Craft's new wood stain formula, the ceramic creations fooled many tourists who thought they really were carved of wood. Ku's image was soon transfigured into Treasure Craft bottle stoppers, wall plaques, mugs, and ashtrays.

Sensuous and shapely, Guerrero's undulating hula dancers of 1959 were a natural addition to the Latin dancer lines made in California. A traditional *Hula Girl* wore a form fitting white crackle painted dress, while the *Royal Hawaiian Hula Dancer* swayed in the revealing grass *pa'u* popularized in the post-missionary revival of hula. Treasure Craft's hula figurines were a premium line in their day, retailing for $10 a pair.

Treasure Craft ceramic *Ki'i* ("tiki gods") representing the war god Ku were often mistaken for wood. Guerrero first carved these into clay in 1959, 11" and 8.5", $65-75 and $40-45.

Hawaiian themes were a favorite sketch topic for Al Levin over the years, inspiring several new designs in Kahului.

50 Treasure Craft of Hawaii: 1959-1984

Ku low ashtray, c. 1960, 3.5", $20-22.

Accompanying Treasure Craft's hula wahine were an *Ul'i Ul'i* gourd shaking boy, and a seated Drummer Boy beating the large *pahu* hula drum used in traditional religious ceremonies. Guerrero's skillful depictions were powerfully muscular, the drum well detailed, and their chocolaty skin offset by white crackle contrasts.

While the Royal Hawaiian and *Drummer Boy* came only in the large size, the other duo could also be purchased in a smaller size more convenient for travelers. Ironically, Guerrero's trademark facial abstractions were evocative of the older hula figures of the Hawaiian Potters Guild, though there was no link between the two firms.

Uli Uli Boy and Hula Girl figurines were recast in a more portable size for tourists, c. 1960, $30-35/ea.

The plant opened just before statehood, in early 1959. A dozen Maui locals were hired and trained to replicate all the functions of the mainland factory. Clay was shipped from Los Angeles, then blended on site and cast into molds created from hydrocal dies cast on Maui. After finishers trimmed mold lines, decorators painted on white crackle glazes, rubbed wood stain into highlights and brushed the brown glaze over entire pieces, accentuating the crackling. Items were hand packed and shipped inter-island.

The new venture was clearly intended to promote pride in Hawaiian skill and craftsmanship. Many Compton designed molds (including seahorse wall pockets and fish ashtrays) were also used in Maui, wearing hang tags that proclaimed, "What Hawaii Makes, Makes Hawaii. This item was manufactured on…Maui by skilled HAWAIIANS."

Sales started slowly. Jet travel to Hawaii had just begun, and the tourist boom that would soon feed the Kahului plant was nascent. Accounts were limited to local variety stores, military post exchanges, and the House of Coral.

Seahorse wall pocket, a Compton mold reworked in Hawaii in 1959, 6.75", $22-25.

A 1959 hang tag proclaiming the virtues of Hawaiian industry was used just briefly. Hang tags have proven to add value to figurines.

Levin responded as he had in California, seeking to expand Treasure Craft's Hawaiian lines in many directions. He sketched endless *tapa* designs, based on authentic Hawaiian bark cloth patterns and textures; these were then sculpted as borders for numerous serving and ash trays, shaped as papayas, pineapples, and fish. *Beachwood*, a driftwood-styled border, morphed into a canister set, with chains hanging ceramic nameplates from their pineapple finials, denoting coffee, tea, flour, and sugar.

Treasure Craft of Hawaii: 1959-1984

Fish ashtrays changed as they migrated to Hawaii, 3". Red, South Gate, 1956, $20-24. Walnut, Compton, 1957, $10-12. Textured, Hawaii, 1959, $14-16.

Ray Murray's Hawaiian Designs

Seeking more designs, Levin hired esteemed pottery designer Ray Murray to manage the new plant. Best known for creating Bauer's *Cal Art* and *Gloss Pastel* wares around 1940, he'd also designed Frankoma's famous Indian chief in headdress, buffalo, and hound dog figures in the 1930s. For Murray, moving to Hawaii fulfilled a lifelong dream, and he took to the new position with enthusiasm.

Murray brought several lines into being for Treasure Craft of Hawaii during his three-year stint, including a realistic *Coconut* line of tableware and calabash bowls, the famed *Lei Footprint Handi-Tray* and the pineapple shakers that evolved into an entire line of pineapple shaped serving pieces. To commemorate Hawaiian statehood, Murray's *50th State* wares included the woven *Lauhalu* pineapple frond tray and the *Driftwood* tray that would serve as a Treasure Craft souvenir blank for decades.

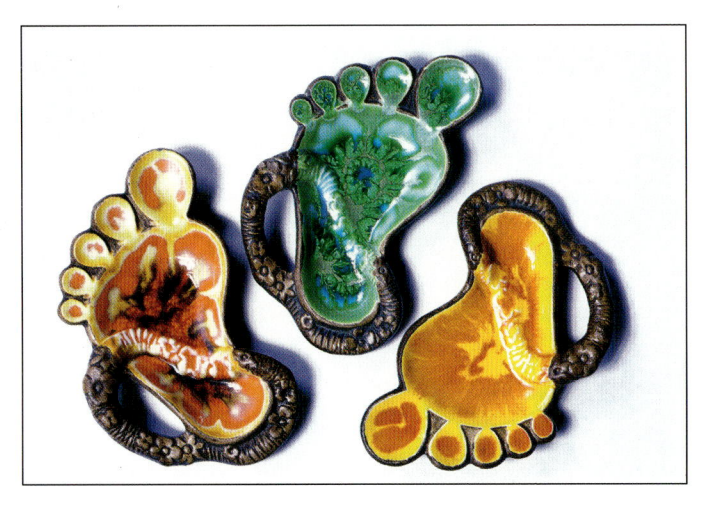

Ray Murray designed Bauer's Cal Art and Frankoma's Indian Chief twenty-five years before he became the Maui plant's manager. Lei Footprint Handi-Tray is his most recognized Treasure Craft of Hawaii design, 1962, 4.5", $15-18/ea.

Along with his California counterpart, Tom Phillips, manager Murray introduced Treasure Craft's new multicolor glazing technique to the Hawaiian plant. Thin lines of beads of one powdered enamel color were laid over another, then kiln melted to create a kaleidoscopic effect. These controlled glazes swirled into striking colors, well suited for the naturalistic leaf tray designs that soon populated the Kahului facility.

Croton and taro, monstera and banana leaves were decorated in the new colors. Some of the vibrant hues were naturalistic matches for Hawaiian flora, others fantastically psychedelic. Leaf shapes began to deepen into *pu pu* dishes, suitable for all varieties of snacks.

Murray and Compton manager Tom Phillips introduced Peacock and other controlled, variegated glazes to the Hawaiian lines in the early '60s.

Coconut sugar bowl and spoon, Murray design, c. 1960, 3.5", $18-20.

52   Treasure Craft of Hawaii: 1959-1984

Hawaii became the 50th state just after the plant opened, and Murray celebrated it on the Driftwood tableware blanks. Tray, 8", $14-16.

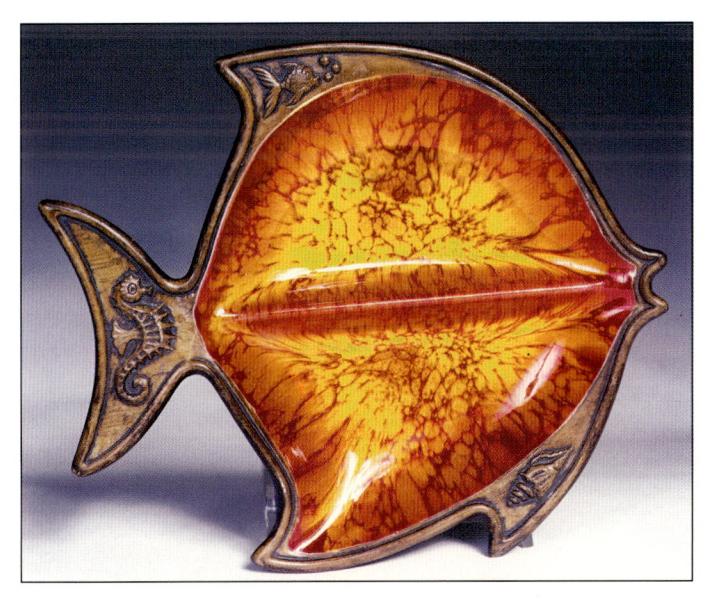

Fish divided *pu pu* dish in Red, #399, 1960s, 8.5", $20-24.

Surf Culture Sweeps the Mainland

Tourism began to swell in 1960s Hawaii, and Treasure Craft's switch from the Sultan sales force to independent Morey Fogel paid off when the upscale Liberty House and tony new hotels in Maui's new Kaanapali resort district placed orders. Large, detailed figurines like the *Mouse Troubadours* and the *Chinese Busts, Emperor and Empress* statues were discontinued in favor of small items that tourists could easily take home. The palm with hanging coconuts shaker set soon became the Hawaiian plant's top seller, followed by salt and pepper fish, ships, tourists, and a pirate skull with treasure chest. A large number ended up going home with Japanese travelers (a trend Hawaiian antique shop owners say has continued).

Menehune, c. 1961. Seated on Oahu chest, 4.5", $22-25. Seated, 3.5", $10-12. Recumbent, 4.5", $13-16.

Coconut palm shaker set, Hawaii's best seller, 1960s, 5.75", $12-16.

Treasure Craft's elfin Sprites had provided the firm its earliest success in the 1940s, and the Maui factory's five styles of *Menehune* represented the Hawaiian equivalent. Legend claimed these gnome-like creatures predated the Polynesians, coming out of their forest caves at night to produce unusual stonework and create playful mischief. Since humans could not see them, Treasure Craft took creative license, making them cuter and less stubby than Hawaiian lore described. Hang tags proclaiming their origins were worn by most of the wood stained Menehune figures.

Treasure Craft of Hawaii: 1959-1984   53

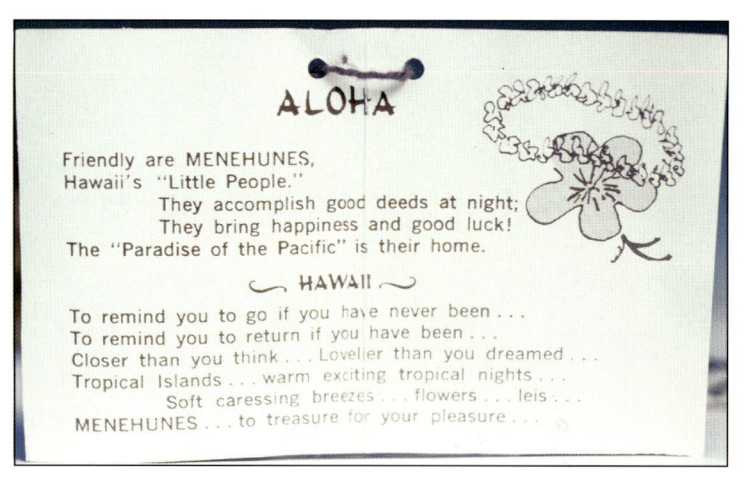

Menehune legend tag, c. 1960s.

Surf culture swept America in the early '60s, and suddenly, the Hawaiian plant's styles were popular all over America. The Hawaiian plant started shipping to the mainland, and its figurines and trays sold rapidly in the Hawaiian Pavilion at the 1962 Seattle World's Fair.

Mainland distribution of the Hawaiian designs had a huge impact on the California parent company. Demand ran so high that Compton started producing pineapple and leaf trays in huge amounts, their marks retooled to reflect their California origins. Ray Murray saw opportunity, leaving Treasure Craft in 1963 to make similar wares in Honolulu under the Tiki Isle and Hana Isle names.

Pineapple Handi-Trays, #40, c. 1963, 5.5", $10-15/ea.

Managing Maui's Sudden Success

Trained in ceramics at Maui High, Murray's 25-year-old assistant, Clarence De Coite, took over the plant. "It was a very demanding job," he remarked. "We were so busy that the Compton plant started shipping us pieces pre-glazed with the colors so they'd only have to be wood stained," he added. But it was the Hawaiian-made items that held cache with the tourists; every item hand worked in Kahului began to bear an oval foil *Made in Hawaii* label. (A *Hawaiian Manufacturer's Association Member* label followed in later years.)

Even adding seasonal help didn't fill the demand some years, due in part to the dilapidation of the decades-old building. "Before professional pest control, the coconut trees would attract rats, so we shut down and sprayed poison out of the hoses we used to lacquer the figurines." After the line was cleared and restarted, the rats fled into the building to perish. "We had to shut down again while we moved all the kilns and mold racks to remove the rats."

Building security was another trouble. "Kids would break in and paint moustaches and goatees on the hula figurines at night with the crackle paint!" De Coite laughed. To his knowledge, none of these self-styled variants were allowed to leave the plant. Staff also complained throughout the plant's history of hearing voices, objects shifting place, and other signs of supernatural presences in the old metal building.

A school of "bubble" fish, Flame, Peacock, and Yellow, #28, c. 1965, 9.5", $20-24/ea.

A greater threat to security was the theft of designs and production techniques, particularly by Japanese pottery makers. "We had to quit letting tourists visit the plant after we found copies cast from one of our leaf molds in Woolworth's," De Coite stated. "Mr. Levin told the maker they could sell what was left, but that they'd better never make another, and they didn't." After that, all molds were carefully destroyed when they became dull from use.

54 Treasure Craft of Hawaii: 1959-1984

Fortunately for modern collectors, the knockoffs never quite matched Treasure Craft's wood staining and highlighting techniques. Whether from Japan or other California firms, most suffered from blotchiness, or were blandly, evenly brown. "The people in the plant who knew how to mix it were sworn to secrecy, and carried it to their graves," spoke Annette Psyck, who started as a seasonal worker in her high school years and would later manage the plant.

New Lines in '69

New designs were introduced on De Coite's watch in 1969. *Keiki* boy and girl hula dancers were added in two sizes, along with a restyled drummer and hula Wahine, their longer hair in step with the styles of the new hippie population that moved to the island that year.

An engagingly flat-faced *Maori* fertility god line had fared poorly in the pre-tourist era, so Levin instead introduced a new ki'i representing *Lono*, the Hawaiian god of good fortune. A handful of samples were glazed in a matte lava black, an experiment prompted by the success of the cast lava ki'i Ray Murray was now designing for Coco Joe's; but production lines were apparently only done in wood stain.

Maori fertility god, Guerrero design, scarce, c. 1960, 11.5", $100-125.

Keiki hula dancers, c. 1969, 11". White lei done as samples only. Samples, $70-80/ea. Brown, $30-35/ea.

De Coite and brother Henry were the last to make molds in Maui, which would be shipped from Compton in later years. De Coite's biggest design contribution was a new back stamp. On receiving an early leaf die with no mark of origin, he hand-scratched a "MADE IN HAWAII" mark in a crude, overlying stick fashion into the master mold. "It turned out visitors wanted things authentically made in Hawaii with a handmade look," De Coite mused; sales rose 10% based on the small change, and the hand-scribed mark soon embellished most of the line.

Tapa border abstract two-section fish tray, Guerrero, c. 1959, 12.5", $45-50.

The De Coite brothers exemplified the feeling of *ohana* among Treasure Craft staff on Maui...many of the workers were indeed family members. After working through Treasure Craft's most feverish years, De Coite and his brother moved on to Maui Cement, a company desperate to keep up with the isle's unprecedented building boom. Psyck's aunt Caroline Casala became plant manager, and her mother worked for Treasure Craft as well. Couples first met at the plant, and celebrations were frequent, as Jeanette Levin recounted. "Every time I went, someone was having a birthday party! Al used to visit the plant every month, and they all spent time talking about anything and everything."

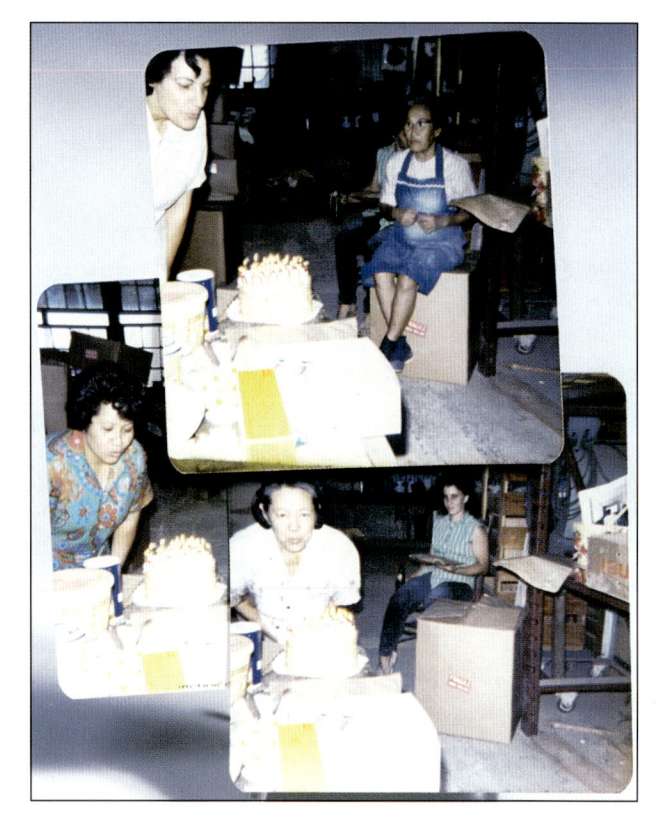

Plant staff even helped Levin stage the first ever Hawaiian Seniors Golf Tournament, which he turned into an annual event on Maui. (Reluctantly succumbing to women's lib, he added a ladies' match in the 1970s.) Levin became part of one business hui after another, and his continued interest in Treasure Craft of Hawaii led him to buy out the share controlled by L.A. Potteries in the late '60s.

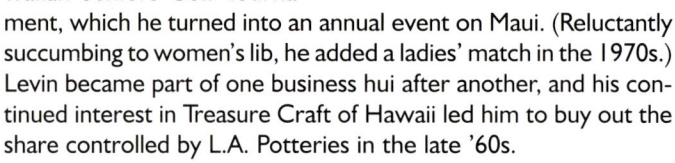

The feeling of *ohana* among the Treasure Craft of Hawaii family shows in these photos of Flora Martin, Salomi Brown, and Hisako Mukai celebrating birthdays at the plant, c.1970s.

Growth and Change in the 1970s

More new lines surfaced on 1970s sales sheets...tapa patterned lighters and ashtrays and desk sets, shell shaped gum savers, volcano shaped bowls, and a line of mugs translating the English titles of family members into Hawaiian. Even as its parent firm struggled in the '70s economy, Treasure Craft of Hawaii sold well as the populations of residents and tourists exploded on Maui; even the local American Savings Bank branches ordered pieces as premiums. In retrospect, the Hawaiian souvenirs gained huge exposure at a critical time for the parent firm, which soon added nameplates of hundreds of American tourist attractions to shell bowls, fruit trays, and pin dishes once sold only in the Aloha State.

Ki'i representing *Kono* god of good fortune, introduced c. 1969. Ray Murray had gone on to successfully create Coco Joe's reconstituted lava figures, so a few Treasure Craft "tiki gods" were given an experimental lava black glaze. Rare, $200-250.

Flower power surgeon fish tray, late 1960s, 8.75", $15-20.

Hawaiian Greetings paperweights, c. 1970s. (The same figures were also sold as cork bottle stoppers.) $10-15/ea.

Dole Kids advertising bell, late 1970s, 3.75", $14-18.

But as the '70s waned, big changes were in store for Treasure Craft, and the outmoded Hawaiian plant was ill-equipped to move with them. Souvenirs were now glazed antique white on the mainland, bearing decals of sailboats and butterflies, or the popular new Dole Kids decal. The new lines required equipment Kahului lacked, leaving the Hawaiian plant little to do but label, pack, and ship.

Maui offered so many new employment options that the industrial wages Treasure Craft had to pay made the plant uncompetitive with mainland production. Yet loyalty between the Levins and their staff kept the operation producing some figurines, and the remaining work was shared. "Everyone really had to be able to do everything" was a sentiment shared by De Coite and Psyck.

Experiments and Prototypes

Hawaiian decorators experimented, adding gold leaf to some pieces, and white crackle trim to the lei of the keiki and restyled hula figures. A few pairs of the original Drummer Boy and Hula Girl were dressed in captivating orange and white swirls. Psyck took these variants to the Honolulu gift show each May, and on her sales rounds through Maui. They attracted attention and boosted orders for the regular lines, but none made it into the line as production items. (Collector confusion over these scarce prototypes grew after the Tom Hanks movie Volcano Joe featured Treasure Craft hula dancers as lamp bases, but these proved to have been grafted on after market by tourists.)

Psyck's 1984 decision to move to Kona on the big island fell concurrently with Treasure Craft's decision to discontinue all wood stain production. With no heir apparent to develop and sell new lines, closure was certain. After the summer tourist peak ended, Treasure Craft of Hawaii ceased production. Psyck faithfully executed Al Levin's command that all molds in the Kahului factory be destroyed.

Hawaii remained an important sales area for Treasure Craft. The Hawaiian foil labels were initially attached to some mid-1980s California ware, which proved easy to distinguish from truly Hawaiian production by their solid colors under clear overglaze. Liberty House continued to order through the 1990s, notwithstanding the irony of seeing the Pueblo inspired *Origins* coiled basket for sale in Honolulu.

Drummer Boy and Hula Girl prototypes with experimental orange glaze, c. 1970s. Not produced, rare. No established value.

Treasure Craft of Hawaii: 1959-1984

Epilogue: The Hawaiian Fantasies Story

Al Levin's interest in Hawaii never waned. He maintained a home in Sprecklesville, and partnerships in real estate, including the Iao Needle Hotel.

Forgotten was the old A&B warehouse in Kihei, where a small number of early 1960s molds were discovered and dug from the surrounding grounds in 1993. A few were brought to Charles Powell, who'd started Hawaiian Fantasies pottery with his wife and daughter in Makawao three years prior.

Powell's pottery made diving dolphin figurines, boxes shaped like outrigger canoes, and various other ocean themed ceramics, selling to Lamonts department stores and hotel gift shops in Hawaii, Guam, and Saipan. Powell realized what Treasure Craft had learned: "Made in Maui was important to the buyers. It was what we had going for us."

So when he encountered the Treasure Craft pineapple and turtle bowl molds, he was eager to apply his airbrush decorating effects to them. His search for their owner led to a Treasure Craft collector in Wailuku, accountant Lloyd Kimoura. A longtime friend and business partner of Al Levin's, Kimoura arranged a meeting between Powell and Levin in 1994.

Levin commented that more molds might exist in the old storehouse and encouraged Powell to look. Though most were water damaged beyond recognition, a handful more were rescued. Certain styles of Menehunes, a three leaf pu pu server, a fish dish, some Handi-Trays, even the scarce Mouse troubador and a Chinese woman bust were discovered. Also found was a short-lived *Elemakule* dresser valet, the old man holding a banana leaf (for keys or coins) and sitting on a hidden wallet cache.

Levin visited Powell's three-kiln operation, located in a former 1910s slaughterhouse in Makawao. "He was a really nice old man," Powell retold. "We were the only Hawaiian ceramicists doing airbrush decorating on shore creature figurines, and he liked the effect. He suggested we try it on some of the molds, and see how it turned out."

Powell's airbrush colors ran to happy pastels, yellows, greens, tan, and deep pink hues. Pineapples were brushed in colors suggestive of nature, while Menehunes were painted in styles similar to Treasure Craft's 1940s Sprites. Turtle bowls wore deep green over brushed black and brown mottling. Though the Treasure Craft mark was masked in some castings, it showed through the white clays and glazes on others.

This entirely different treatment of Treasure Craft's 1960s lines gave them a fresh, modern look. Levin liked the results, and recommended that Powell test the market. Hang tags and labels indicating their Maui origin were added, and the initial run was sent to stores.

Turtle with black and brown airbrush. Perhaps a few hundred were made from recovered Treasure Craft molds, 1994, 8.5", $20-24.

Hawaiian Fantasies outrigger canoe box, c. 1990. Predates rediscovery of the Treasure Craft molds. Foil label on bottom, used sporadically.

Menehune with airbrushing bears remarkable resemblance to c. 1950 Treasure Craft novelties. 1994, 4.5", $19-24.

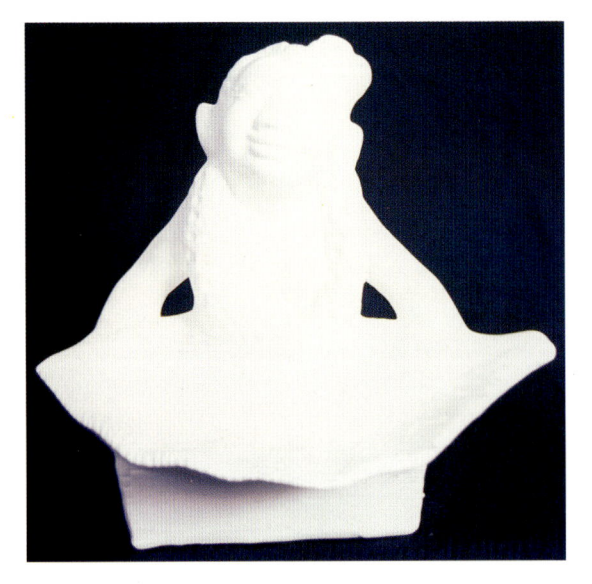

After Al Levin's passing in 1995, Hawaiian Fantasies removed the *elemakule* (old man) dresser valet and all other Treasure Craft molds from production.

Hawaiian Icons

Treasure Craft's in-mold mark still shows on this remake of their pineapple server in pastels, 1994, 10.5", $25-30.

Hawaiian figurines catalogue page, c. 1970.

The updated Treasure Craft designs sold well, and for a brief moment, it appeared that they might be candidates for broad distribution. Sadly though, Levin died in September of 1995, before giving any written approval for such a revival. Out of deference to Mr. Levin, Powell retired the molds to an undisclosed location, and the 2002 closure of Hawaiian Fantasies removed any chance of their reproduction. The few hundred 1995 pieces made have rarely surfaced in Treasure Craft collections.

Elemakule dresser valet, Guerrero design, c. 1959. Banana leaf held keys and coins, opening beneath figure held wallet.

Rear detail of shorter Keiki Dancers, c. 1969, 7.5", $20-25/ea.

Treasure Craft of Hawaii: 1959-1984

Rear view of old man dresser caddy, 8.5" x 8". Costly and cumbersome for tourists to carry, they didn't stay in the line for long, $100-125.

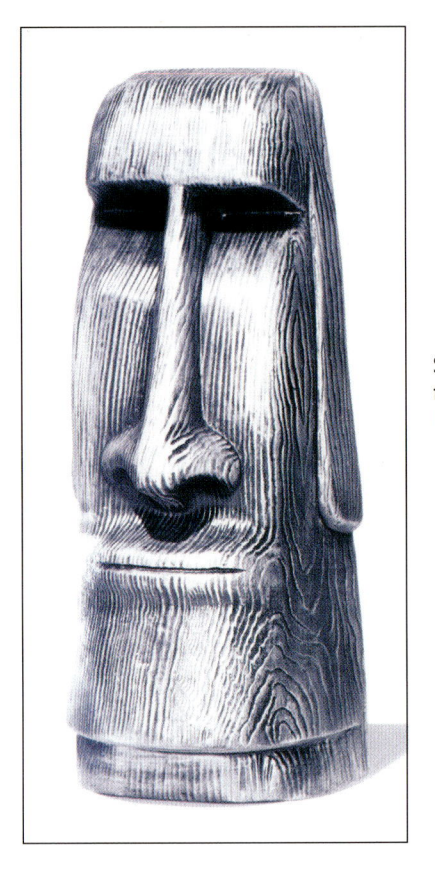

Short-lived stone god head from c. 1960 sales sheet, 11", $95-110.

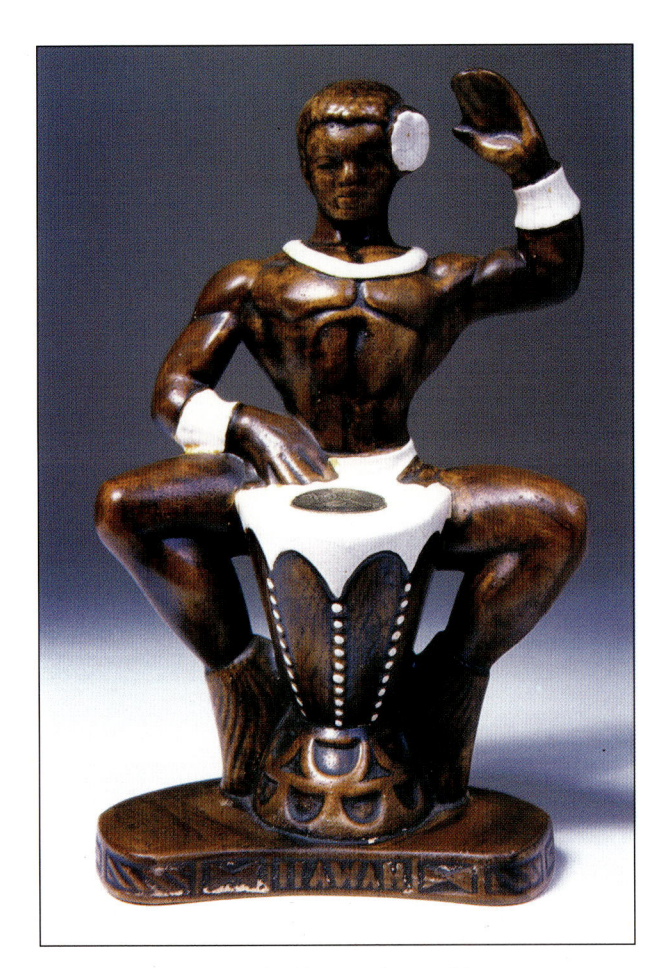

Front view of Treasure Craft's most famous Hawaiian figure, c. 1959. Art director Tony Guerrero's emphasis on motion and carriage followed from his stylish Latin Dancers series of the late '50s.

Most Mouse Troubadours came from Compton, but some were made on Maui. Cellist, gold leaf and cold-painted eyes, c. 1959. Hawaii mark, $50-55. Compton mark, $40-45.

60   Treasure Craft of Hawaii: 1959-1984

Hula trio with Royal Hawaiian *olapa* (dancer), c. 1959.

Two views of Royal Hawaiian dancer, made in 11.5" size only, $50-60.

Treasure Craft of Hawaii: 1959-1984   61

Arms were applied with clay slip to the bodies by the finishers, and occasionally ended up in different positions.

Restyled hula wahine, Guerrero design. White skirt and lei differentiate scarce samples from production pieces, which were all brown, c. 1969, 14", $100-125.

Long haired hula wahine and drummer reflected hippie invasion of Maui in 1969. 8", $20-25/ea.

62   Treasure Craft of Hawaii: 1959-1984

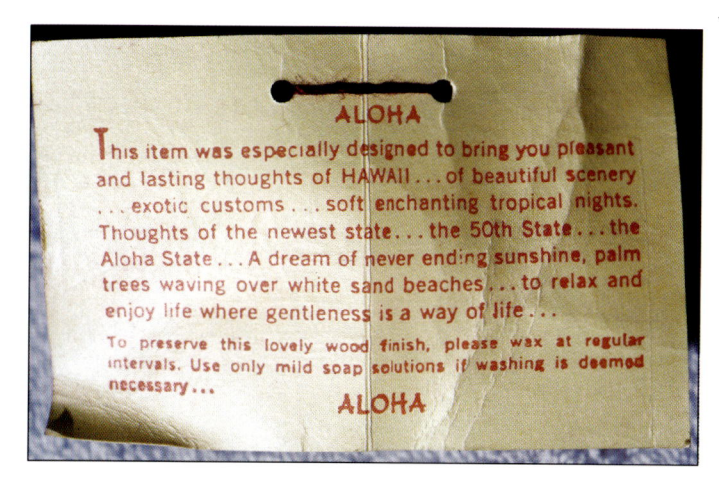

Aloha tag worn by Treasure Craft figurines through most of their production.

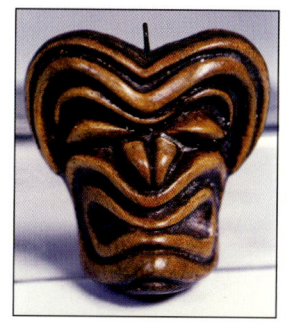

Menehunes and Ki'i masks were suspended as pendants c. 1970, 1.5", $24-28.

Ki'i shakers in base, c. 1960, 4", $15-20.

Tiki Tourist shakers with gold leaf embellishments, c. 1960s, 5.5", $13-16 (more in original box).

Ki'i mug, c. 1960, 4.75", $15-18.

Maori fertility god ashtray, c.1960, 6.25", $25-30.

Treasure Craft of Hawaii: 1959-1984   63

Sea Life

Moorish idolfish four-section fish tray, #398, 1960s, 12", $24-28.

Lei Turtle Handi-Tray, c. 1963, 5.25", $18-24.

Butterfly fish tray, four-section, Heavenly Blue, #390, 1960s, 16.5", $28-35.

Pineapple low pu pu bowl, 1960s, 11.75", $20-27.

Turtle soap dish, 1960s, 7.5", $18-24.

64   Treasure Craft of Hawaii: 1959-1984

Tapa fish Handi-Tray, #43, 1962, 4.25", $15-18.

Lei fish mini tray, c. 1960, 4", $12-15.

Seahorse tray in Lime, c. 1970, 8", $12-15.

Fish wall pocket from a Compton mold sent to Hawaii, c. 1959, 6.5", $20-25.

Treasure Craft of Hawaii: 1959-1984   65

Monstera Leaves

Monstera leaf ashtray in original white crackle glaze, #31, c. 1959, 12", $20-25.

Stemless Monstera variant, c. 1960s, 11", $16-20.

Monstera ashtray in original shrink wrap, naturalistic green, #29, c. 1970, 8.5", $12-18.

Beachwood/Driftwood

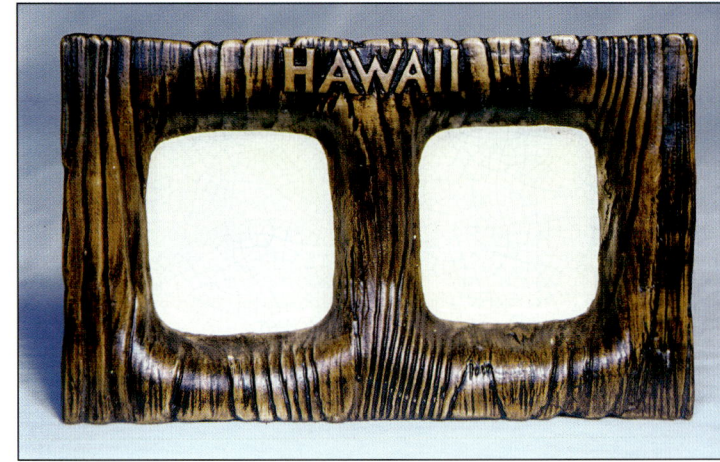

Beachwood double tray, c. 1959, 5.5" x 9.25", $10-15.

Three Driftwood mugs, c. 1960, 4.5". Fish handle, $9-12; Seahorse, $12-15; 50th State, Murray design, $9-12.

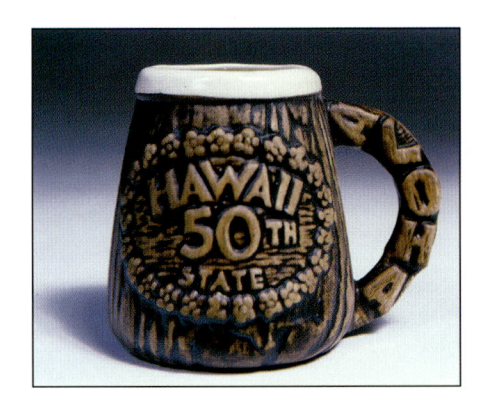

66   Treasure Craft of Hawaii: 1959-1984

Tapa Lines

Stacking ashtray set, c. 1970, 8" and 4", $18-20/set.

Geometric edges derived from Hawaiian bark cloth distinguish the Tapa line. Mini bowl, 1960s, 3.75", $12-14.

Dog bone ashtray, #1920, 1960s, 8", $14-18.

Smoke and snack tray, c. 1959, 9.5", $18-20.

Kidney-shaped mini bowl, #117, c. 1965, 5", $12-15.

Treasure Craft of Hawaii: 1959-1984

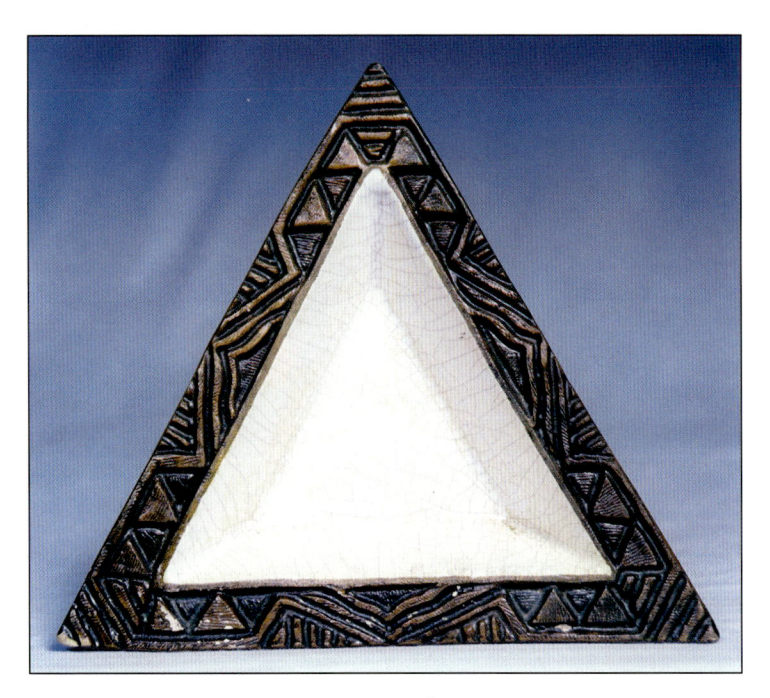

Triangle serving bowl, c. 1959, 7.25", $14-18.

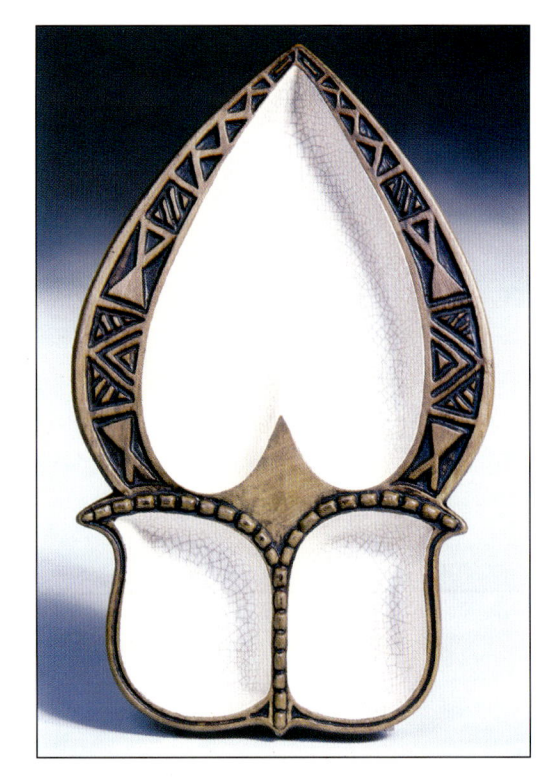

Stylized pod and leaf serving bowl, 1959, 16", $30-35.

Asymmetric ashtray, yellow, 1960s, 9", $12-14.

Diamond divided serving tray (sans handle), c. 1959, $20-24.

Tapa mini bowls, #115/107 (square) and 116 (angular), 1960s, 4", $10-12/ea.

68   Treasure Craft of Hawaii: 1959-1984

Tapa round ashtray, 1960s, 6.75", $14-16.

Desk stand (pens originally included), 50th State, c. 1975, 8.5", $18-20.

Space Age Ashtrays

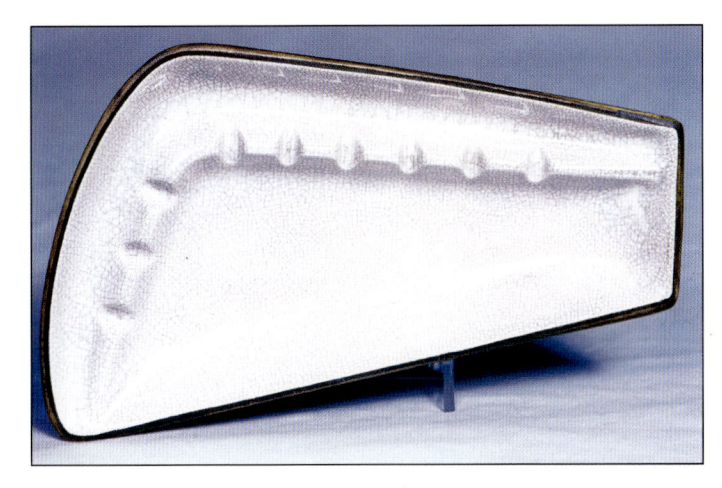

Asymmetric ashtray, #16, 1959, 8.75", $12-15.

Double triangle ashtray, c. 1965, 8.5", $13-16.

Four points ashtray, #17, c. 1965, 6.25", $10-14.

Treasure Craft of Hawaii: 1959-1984   69

Handi-Trays

Handi-Trays were introduced in 1962 with tags proclaiming their catch-all usefulness, 4"-5.5". Croton leaf, $9-12. Pineapple, $10-15. Apple, $8-10. Papaya, $12-15.

Hawaiian Souvenirs

Hawaiian Souvenirs sales sheet, 1970s.

Hawaiian attractions plate, c. 1970, 8", $12-16.

70 Treasure Craft of Hawaii: 1959-1984

Hawaiian hula plate, c. 1970, 6.5", $18-22.

Poi Pounder gourd ashtray or bottle vase, c. 1959, 4.5", $13-15.

Early Novelties

Seldom seen tropical leaf planter, c. 1959, 9", $24-28.

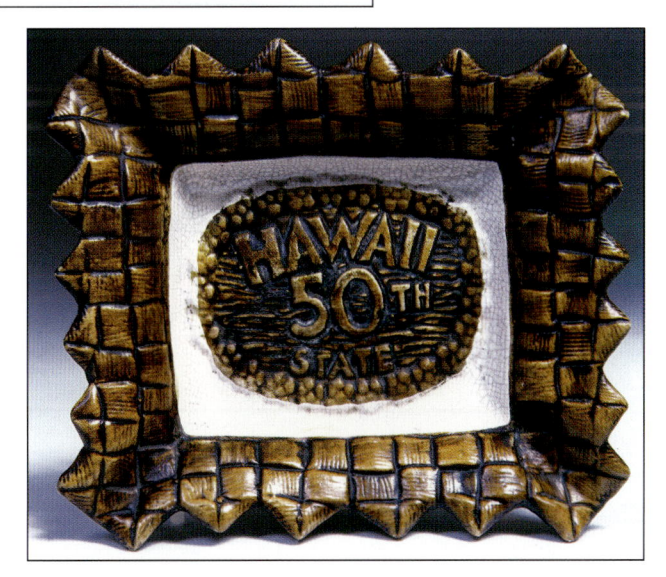

Lauhulu (banana leaf) woven tray with Murray's 50th State emblem, c. 1960, $10-12.

Antique White Hawaiian Ware

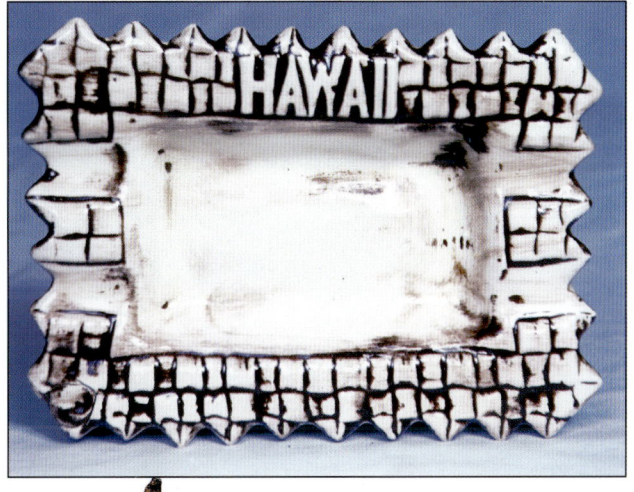

Antique white and decal wares were made on the mainland and processed through the Maui plant by the end of the '70s. Lauhulu tray, c. 1980, 8.75", $5-6.

Treasure Craft of Hawaii: 1959-1984

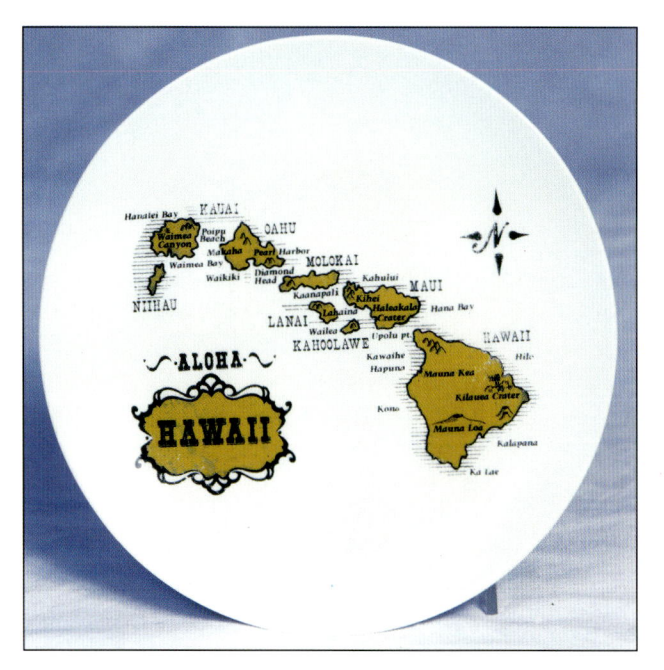

Hawaiian Map decal plate, porcelain (outsourced), 8", c. 1980, $15-18. (Other pieces in line were on Treasure Craft earthenware.)

50th State fish tray in Antique, 1970s, 6.75", $7-9.

Bells, c. 1980, 6.5". Orchids and map, $12-15/ea. Butterfly, $6-8.

Hawaiian Tableware

Pineapple Line bowl, #34, 7", c. 1959, $16-20.

Dole Kids advertising plate or plaque, c. 1980, 8", $16-20.

Menehune on Pineapple bowl, 7", c. 1959, $24-28.

72   Treasure Craft of Hawaii: 1959-1984

Pineapple shakers on banana leaf tray, c. 1959, 4.5" and 6.5", $13-19/set.

Tapa condiment jar, c. 1959, 5", $12-15.

Pineapple shakers in stand, c. 1960s, 4.5", $12-15/set.

Barrel Line dip bowl made on Maui, #143, 1959, 3.5", $6-9.

Tapa mug, c. 1959, 3.5", $6-8.

Ray Murray's departure to set up a competing pottery in Honolulu led Al Levin to mark this Coconut calabash with an unusual A.L. die stamp, 1963, 1.75", $10-15.

Treasure Craft of Hawaii: 1959-1984

Advertising Premiums

This sailboat ashtray in Tangerine was a scarce advertising piece, marked "Napili Kai Beach Club Maui," c. 1965, 6.75", $30-35.

Kona Coffee ad mug and regular small "tiki" mug, c. 1970, 3.5". Kona ad, $15-18; regular, $10-12.

Tapa ad ashtray for Reno restaurant at the height of the '60s Polynesian dining fad, c. 1965, 4.5", $18-22.

74 Treasure Craft of Hawaii: 1959-1984

Hawaiian Shaker Sets

Shaker sets in stands, Ships and Whales, c. 1970, 4.75" and 3.5", $12-18/set.

Shaker sets, c. 1960, Luggage and Treasure Chests, 2.25" and 2.5", $9-11/set.

Treasure Craft of Hawaii: 1959-1984

The Promise of the 1960s

Treasure Craft entered the new decade with understandable optimism. Brisk orders for their wood stain tableware fueled the California plant, and the new Hawaiian figurines wowed a nation feverish over Tiki culture. They became major suppliers to S&H Green Stamp Redemption Centers, and their products now reached an international audience.

Even as Treasure Craft's popularity soared, two of California's "Big Five" potteries, Vernon and Bauer, ceased to exist as independent producers. Dozens of smaller California ceramic factories shuttered, or burned in a series of suspicious fires; their number would shrink from a 1950 peak of around 1000 firms to under 100 by 1969. Modern styles and competitive prices were critical in a market now dominated by Japanese imports.

Treasure Craft proved highly adept at keeping ahead of the market through the '60s, finding simple ways to create complex, hand decorated designs. The company both led and followed popular decorating trends, with new glazes, new figurines, new kitchenware sets, and brand new product lines. The appearance of a Barrel canister set on the kitchen set of *The Dick Van Dyke Show* from 1961-66 heralded the firm's arrival as a major pottery producer.

Calypso Dancer and Drummer, c. 1960, 12.5" and 11.5", $100-125/set.

Barrel Line cookie jar, as seen in the kitchen island on *The Dick Van Dyke Show*, 1961-66, 10.5", $20-25.

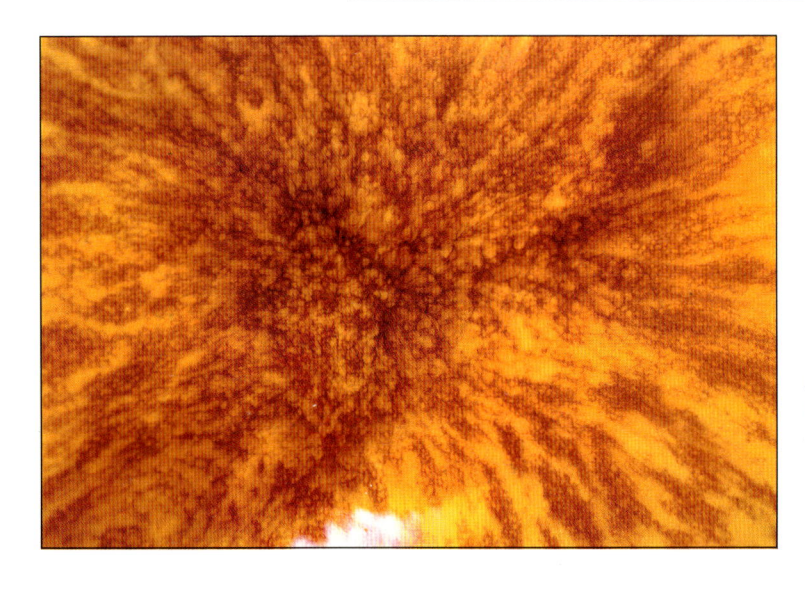

A deeper look into the variegated Red glaze created by Tom Phillips and Tony Guerrero, early 1960s.

New Decorating and Glaze Techniques

Controlled, hand applied glazing was one area where Treasure Craft led 1960s pottery production. Their swirling and spattered glazes, blended in intense colors, anticipated psychedelic '60s motifs years before they swept the nation.

Vivid red and orange, yellow and caramel, lime and olive, orange and yellow combinations were applied to such existing blanks as the *Scroll* ashtray and the four-part square serving tray introduced in 1959. After the interior color was sprayed or bottle painted onto the fired bisque blank, the piece was refired to melt and fuse the colors. Wood stain was then rubbed onto the rims and the underside.

The effect was startling! Comingled colors flowed to the low spots, the lighter colors swirling randomly around dark speckled hues. So for the first time since Sprite production ended in the '50s, Treasure Craft formulated vivid colored glazes.

Experimentation resulted in different blends, depending on how much of one color was used. *Red* could look nearly cherry red, or be heavily speckled with sun orange. Staring into their crystalline depths, they took on a Rorschach blot quality.

The old method of contrasting wood stain with white crackle still held stylish appeal, but the new variegated colors were eye popping and mod. Orders rolled in for existing shapes treated with the new glazes, and a host of new serving ware grew to take advantage of these splashy colors.

Two wild new combinations joined the line by 1963. *Flame* was a tri-color effect, consisting of orange and honey-gold with deep brown centers, while *Peacock* was a soothing combination of green and blue. Decorators became skilled at controlling their application, draping one color around the other to create repeating patterns of cascading color. This would reach its apogee with pieces like the *Butterfly* tray, wings beautifully patterned like that of a Monarch butterfly.

By the late '60s, competitors widely copied the technique, but few mastered it. Treasure Craft kept the concept fresh: some pieces were colored all the way to the rim, leaving no exposed wood stain, while others sported new combinations like *Heavenly Blue*, a controlled blue-lavendar-grey. A few leaf trays were decorated in solid, naturalistic greens (often trimmed in gold); but the kaleidoscopic blended glazes would dominate the market for years.

Butterfly ashtray, Tangerine, #38, c. 1965, 10", $24-27.

Leaf pod server, three-section, c. 1965, #374, 14", $18-22.

Scallop shell chip and dip, c. 1960, 11", $29-36.

The Promise of the 1960s   77

Handi-Trays grew into jumbo servers like this four-section Caricature plant leaf tray. Marked 19©63, but Peacock coloration to edge was a later, less common treatment, #385, 16.5", $24-27.

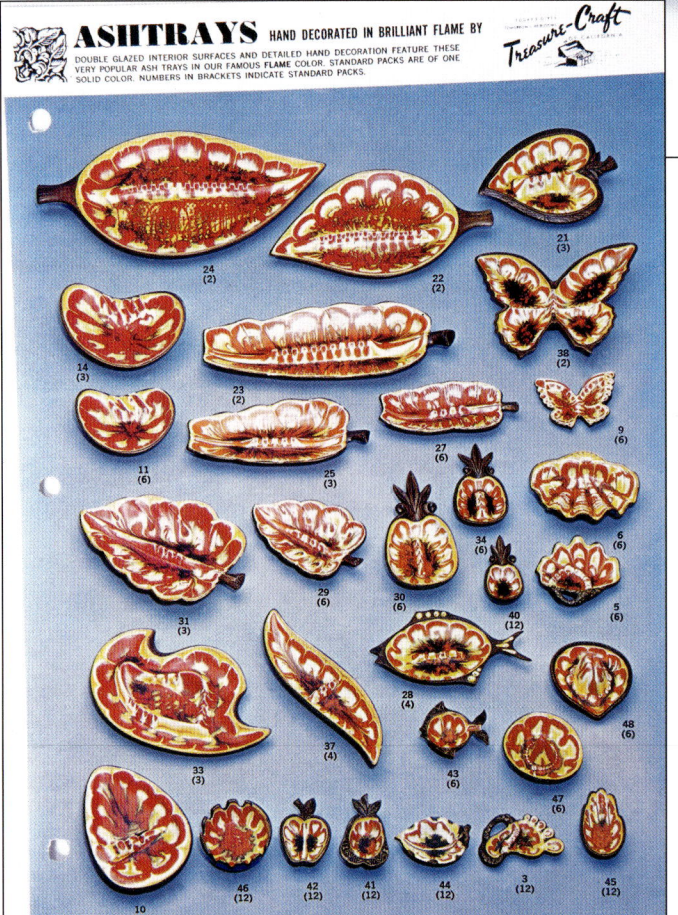

Flame catalog showing controlled glazes on complete range of serving trays, c. 1965.

Guerrero's Fisherman and Lumberjack figures were the first done in monochrome walnut, requiring deeper, more defined sculpting for highlighting. 1962, 14", $45-55/ea.

Figurines

The new colored glazes even found their way to Treasure Craft's newest figurines, the *Calypso Dancers* couple. He wore an orange belt sash, she a pair of orange shoes, earrings, and a multicolored fruit basket headdress. Designed by Tony Guerrero from a concept by owner Al Levin, these were the last in a series of figurines celebrating Latin cultural dances. With the exception of some Hawaiian prototypes, these were Treasure Craft's only wood stained figurines known to have worn a color other than white.

But these would not be the last of Treasure Craft's large wood stain figurines. In 1962, Guerrero and Levin styled laborers with a northern feel, a burly lumberjack and a fisherman clad in rain gear with a large fish on the hook. A smaller series soon followed. These bore no contrasting color decoration; instead, deeply sculpted features that captured the brown glaze more densely offered subtle texture. As with the dancers, Guerrero used great forethought to design attractive, detailed statues that did not require complex molds and applied parts.

78   The Promise of the 1960s

More figurines would be styled for Hawaiian production late in the decade, while Compton crafted smaller novelties. Often highlighted with yellow and white glazes, a pirate head character mug followed from the *Treasure Chest* line of giftware; smaller braying donkey ashtrays, planters, and figurines came around 1963. Guerrero's design flair would eventually be applied to shaker sets of leaping dolphins, rooster letter holders, and a new line of sculptured cookie jars.

By the late '60s, Guerrero was nearing retirement, just as Levin sought to grow the sculptured cookie jar assortment. Levin contacted sculptor/designer Don Winton of the nearby Twin Winton factory, and the two became fast friends. Winton offered more pleasingly fun cookie jar ideas, the start of a 25 year association with Treasure Craft.

Spaniel bank matched cookie jar and canisters, 1961, 9", $18-22.

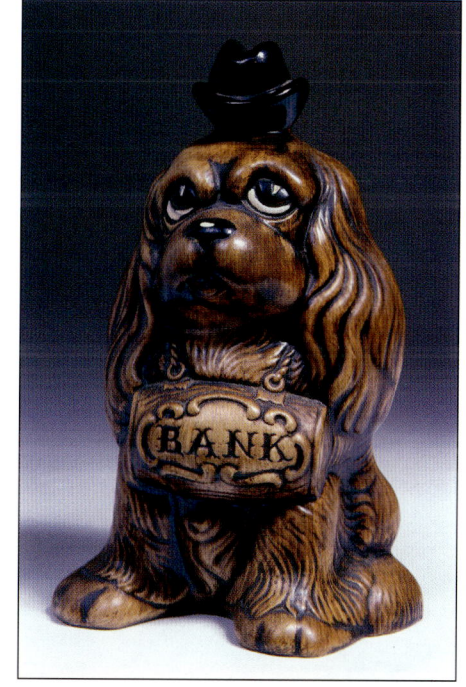

Jackass sculpted planter, 1963, 5.25", $13-16.

Sculptured Novelty Lines

Art director Guerrero's talents were extended to novelty cookie jars in 1960, a smiling chimp with "COOKIES" spelled in round cookie disks across his front. Deeply sculpted details created tonal variations within the wood stain areas, a concept borrowed from the Fruitwood line. Enthusiasm for the animal jar was great and showed that novelty cookie jars could sell separately, without the expense of developing matching kitchenware.

Yet Levin was always eager to extend a good idea into other salable products. The *Spaniel Line* of 1961 included a three-dimensional spaniel in hat, along with canisters and a bank of the same design in different scales. A sculptured hen jar joined the *Rooster Line*, filling out a theme widely desired by circa 1960 kitchen decorators; its eyes and other details were expressively hand-painted.

Origins of novelty cookie jars, 11"-12". Lamb, c. 1968, $25-32. Monkey, c. 1960, $32-40. Baseball Bunny, L.A. Dodgers cap, c. 1965, $45-50. Cat on pillow, c. 1968, $25-32. Spaniel, c. 1961, $28-35.

The Promise of the 1960s

New Tableware

Sculpted designs were by no means limited to cookie jars and novelties at Treasure Craft. The success of Barrel Line and the popularity of the wood stain technique, along with Al Levin's sense of whimsy led him to produce a variety of new tableware lines during the '60s.

Even in his 1980s sketchbooks, Levin dreamt of new revivals for the Naughty Gnomes and Lucky Sprites he first made in the 1940s. The *Leprechaun* line was a 1960 revival that placed these mischievous nymphs as finials or handles on tree trunk butter dishes, cookie jars, shaker sets, and a full line of kitchenware. These detailed and precise pieces wore wood stain, with nameplates deliberately lighter than the rest of the piece. Like their Sprite ancestors, many wore hang tags telling their legend of luck.

Lucky Leprechaun tableware wore hang tags with lore, a Treasure Craft tradition by the time of their early 1960s introduction.

Pineapple Line proved so popular that the California plant had to augment Hawaiian production by 1962. Tray, 8.25". California mark, $12-15; Hawaii mark, $17-19.

Leprechaun resting on butter lid, c. 1960, 5.5", $14-16.

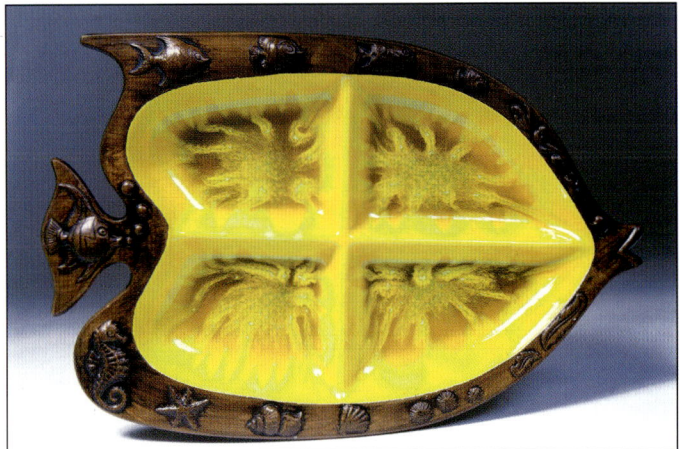

Four-section butterfly fish tray (originally sold with 8" fish dip bowl notched to sit on center cross), #390, c. 1965, 16.5". Tray alone, $24-30.

80   The Promise of the 1960s

Papaya Handi-Tray, later "all-over" Peacock glaze, late '60s, 4.5", $12-15.

Treasure Craft responded in 1961 with the hand-painted *Provincial Line*. Based on Pennsylvania Dutch designs, it included a set of four canisters, which led two courters from singlehood to a kiss. Match safes, a rolling pin wall pocket, and related items gave a country feel, as did red, yellow, and blue details cold-painted over the glaze. Rooster lines were expanded to include canister sets, decorated in colors from yellow and red early in the decade to avocado and honey when those shades moved into late '60s kitchens.

Fruit Line canisters are Treasure Craft's most identifiable items for many non-collectors, c. 1960. Tea and Coffee, 8", $10-14/ea. Flour and Sugar, 9.5", $13-16/ea. Cookies, 10.5", $17-22.

Hawaiian Pineapple was another new 1960 line, designed to match the new Hawaiian plant's production and America's enchantment with coastal living. Shapes derived from the Fruitwood line bore pineapples that popped out in bas relief. Pineapple shaped serving trays nicely offset this wood toned line, wearing the new polychromatic glazes.

Treasure Craft's *Fish Line* became solely devoted to the brilliant new color blends in 1960. From the smallest dip tray to the huge four-part serving tray, every one swam in a sea of dazzling color. Various shapes and sizes received different embossed designs on their rims and tail fins, and homemakers could assemble an impressive school. A natural fit with the sought-after hula dancers, Fish serving ware was made in Maui and California as surf culture swept America.

Fish designs were added to a new variety of *Handi-Trays*, miniature bowls first designed by Hawaiian plant manager and former Bauer Cal-Art designer Ray Murray. Treasure Craft expanded on them in 1962 and 1963, and bare footprint trays were joined by small fruit and leaf styles, occasionally bearing a hang tag proclaiming their usefulness for holding anything from dips to earrings.

These fun, festive patterns found huge acceptance in an era of cocktail culture, as revelers yearned for a simpler life in what became a perplexing decade of social change. But that same impulse made traditional styles representing comfort and stability equally important.

Fruit Line was far and away the biggest smash of Treasure Craft's 1960s tableware. Appearing as tree bark, its impressed fruit designs were highlighted with Treasure Craft's new blended glazes. Pears, apples, and grapes popped out of a wood stump, a three-dimensional effect that found acceptance all over North America. The design proved so popular that nearly every piece made in the huge Barrel Line would come to be styled in Fruit, even the novelty nameplate mugs which launched Treasure Craft's tableware efforts in the 1950s. Fruit would stay in the line through the 1970s; the round canisters, their flat, scrolled tops, adorned with a chrome or plastic finial, have remained Treasure Craft's most identifiable pieces for many people.

Provincial "match safe" wall pocket, c. 1961, 5", $10-12.

The Promise of the 1960s 81

The mid-'60s saw the arrival of two more tableware patterns, *Cavalier* and *Topiary*. A single, manicured flower ball in a solid color suited Topiary to the flower power generation, while Cavalier boasted a noble courtier textured into a wood stain panel. These were relatively short-lived, though some scrolled and floral embossed trays in the blended colors outlived the canister sets in these limited lines.

sombrero tray doubled as a ring holder, while Washington apple bowls and spoon rests from Milwaukee served enough function to offer value beyond that of travel memento.

More function meant more display space, and Treasure Craft dramatically broadened the nameplate items gift shops could order throughout the '60s. Vases, napkin holders, banks, lighters, bells, picture frames, shakers, and desk accessories all came to be eligible for the treatment. Collected by tourists worldwide, these items would help the firm survive the rocky times that lay just ahead.

Nameplate Line of souvenirs, late 1960s. Not shown elsewhere: Napkin holders, 4.5", $12-16/ea. Skillet plaques, 8.5", $8-10/ea. Trays, various, $8-12/ea.

Cavalier Line undulating ashtray in Heavenly Blue, c. 1965, 13", $14-18.

Souvenirs

Vernon Kilns 1958 merger with Metlox left a void in the souvenir market, which Treasure Craft quickly helped fill. Visitors to Hawaii included owners of attractions in the lower forty-eight states, who spotted Treasure Craft's Maui-made figurines, pineapple bowls, and small trays all over the islands. Demand for similar items surged, but the cost to produce unique wares for each locale would have been prohibitive.

Met with this sudden demand, the Compton plant developed a *Nameplate Line*. Attractions anywhere could have their name cast as a ceramic medallion, which would then be fused to many of Treasure Craft's smaller trays, bowls, and shakers. Theme parks from Knott's Berry Farm to Tampa's Tiki Gardens could easily sell the minimum assortment of 500 pieces, and Treasure Craft soon enjoyed national exposure at tourist traps in all fifty states.

Nameplates were made for every state, and most major American cities. Yellowstone Park ordered bears, Cape Cod a whale, and alligators sold with a Florida escutcheon. An Arizona

Florida shell and fish tray, c. 1970, 5", $10-15.

Shaker sets were name-plated for attractions in all fifty states. Bear and Beehive shakers in stand, c. 1970, 4.25", $10-13.

Caricature plant leaf four-section server, #385, c. 1963, 16.5", $15-20.

The End of an Era

By the end of the '60s, Treasure Craft's success had brought new pressures. California Originals, Santa Anita Ware, Maddux, Freeman-McFarlin, Maurice of California, Dorrance, American Bisque, and other American and Japanese potteries were emulating Treasure Craft's wood stain, some even issuing faithful copies of Treasure Craft items. The stay-at-home housewife, who planned frequent parties and redeemed grocery stamps for the necessary serving ware, was an endangered species. So was the California pottery industry.

Colorful Trays

Taro leaf style four-section server, chipmunk border, c. 1965, 17.5", $18-22.

Floral embossed serving platter, #395, c.1965, 17.5", $18-22.

The Promise of the 1960s   83

Center handled two-section leaf server, c. 1965, 5.5" x 10", $14-18.

Apple chip and dip (also available as two separate nesting bowls), c. 1965, 17", $18-22.

Butterfly ashtray in striking Red, #38, 1960s, 10", $24-27.

Teardrop ashtray, c. 1963, 9", $15-20.

84   The Promise of the 1960s

Server Line catalog page in Heavenly Blue, late 1960s. This color was introduced well after the controlled Flame and Peacock combinations, so is less common. Items not shown elsewhere: Large four-and-five-section trays, $20-24/ea. Other medium leaf and pod bowls and trays, $14-18/ea. Small three-section pu pu dish, #378, $11-14.

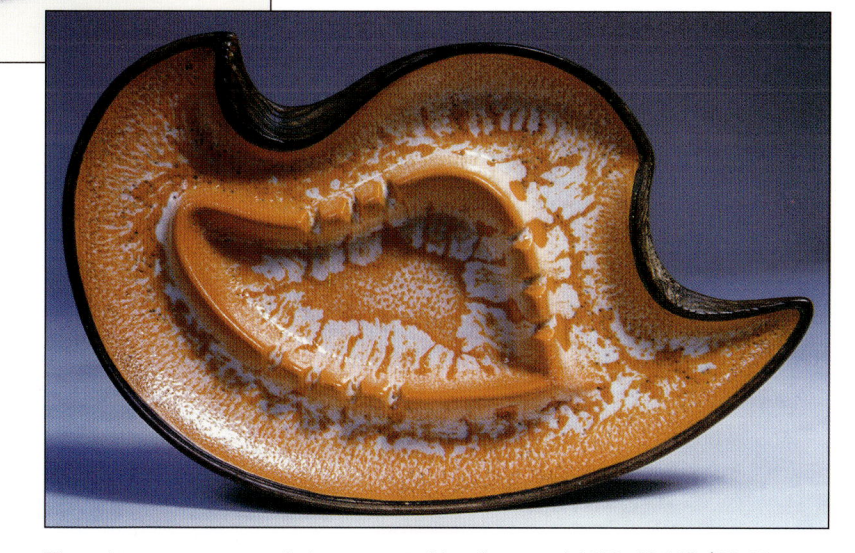

Against a neutral background, the true colors of Heavenly Blue show through in this two-section leaf pod bowl, #376, late 1960s, 12.75", $14-18.

This white on orange peel glaze was tried briefly around 1970, 12.25", $12-15.

The Promise of the 1960s   85

Surf Culture and Hawaiian Influences

Fish four-section tray, #397, 1960s, 20", $30-35.

Abstract fish coin tray in Lime glaze, c. 1970, 5.5", $12-14.

Banana leaf ashtray, naturalistic colors, gold trim, c. 1970, 17.5", $18-24/ea.

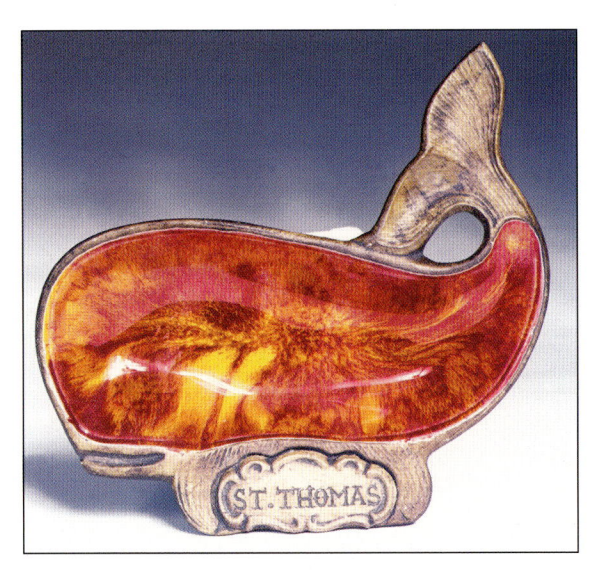

Whale tray with souvenir nameplate from Virgin Islands, late 1960s, 7", $13-16.

Baby butterfly fish tray, Oregon nameplate. These were originally designed without nameplates to sit as dip bowls in the center of the #390 butterfly fish four-section tray. #391, 1960s, 7", $8-12/ea.

Gum Savers, hand and footprints, 1960s, 3", $12-15/ea.

Hand print Handi-Trays were made in both California and Hawaii, c. 1962, 4", $10-14/ea.

Fish planter, c. 1960, 4.25" x 7", $12-16.

Monstera leaf ashtray with later "all over" glazing (backs were still wood stained), c. 1965, 8.5", $14-16.

The Promise of the 1960s 87

1960s Table and Kitchen Ware

Though Menehune figures were made in Hawaii, the Compton plant grafted them to leftover hors d' oeuvres centerpieces from their mid-'50s lines. Pineapple, 7", $12-18; Christmas Tree, 6.5", $16-20; Bare Tree, 7", $12-15.

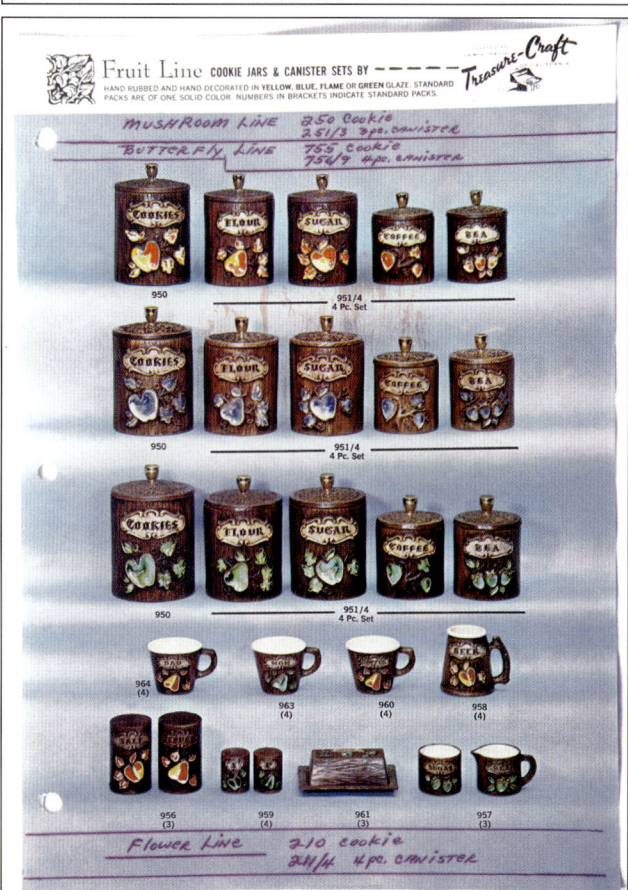

Fruit Butter dish/lid, c. 1960s, $10-15.

Fruit Line sold well during its fifteen year run. Items not shown elsewhere:
- Canister, Cookie, $15-18.
- Canister, Sugar or Flour, $12-14.
- Canister, Coffee or Tea, $10-12.
- Creamer, $6-8.
- Cup, $5-7.
- Mug, $7-9.
- Shakers, table, $5-6.
- Sugar, $4-6.

Fruit Shakers, range size, 5", c. 1960s, $8-10/pr.

88   The Promise of the 1960s

Pineapple mug, c. 1960, 6", $6-8.

Pineapple mug prototype, multi-color with overglaze, c. 1970. Never produced.

Provincial Line five canister set, c. 1961, $45-60/set.

Pineapple Line ad slick, c. 1960. Items not shown elsewhere:
Canister, Coffee and Tea, $22-28/ea.
Canister, Cookie, $35-40.
Canister, Sugar and Flour, $25-30/ea.
Chip and two dips, $20-25.
Pitcher, juice, $20-24.
Tray, Menehune, 11.75", $22-25.

Cavalier Line sold for just a few years, c. 1965.

Lucky Leprechaun ware, introduced 1960. Sugar/lid with spoon, 4.5", $12-15. Creamer, 4", $12-15. Salt and Pepper, 4.75", $15-18/set.

The Promise of the 1960s   89

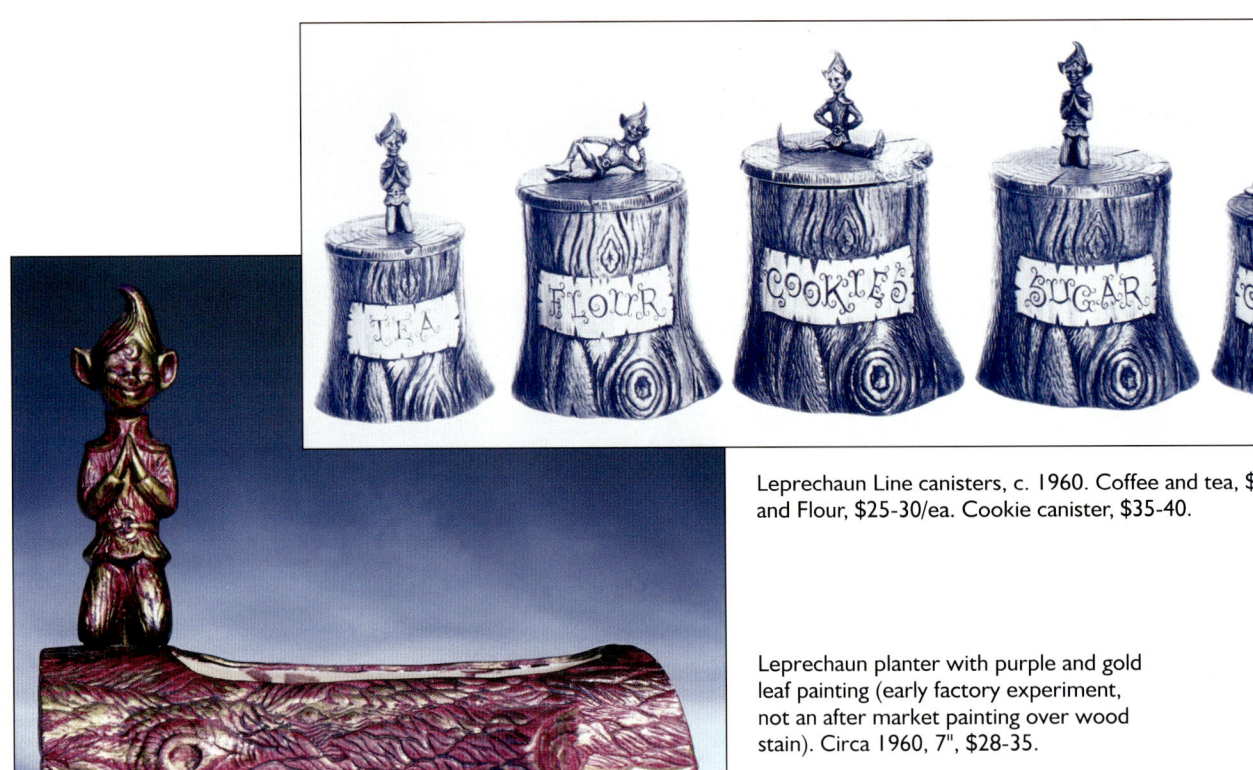

Leprechaun Line canisters, c. 1960. Coffee and tea, $22-28/ea. Sugar and Flour, $25-30/ea. Cookie canister, $35-40.

Leprechaun planter with purple and gold leaf painting (early factory experiment, not an after market painting over wood stain). Circa 1960, 7", $28-35.

Treasure Chest shakers, c. 1960, 4", $14-18/set.

Treasure Chest butter/lid, c. 1960, 7.5", $18-24.

Rooster and hen motifs were an early '60s favorite. Napkin holder, 7.5", $10-14.

90   The Promise of the 1960s

Sculpted Novelty Lines

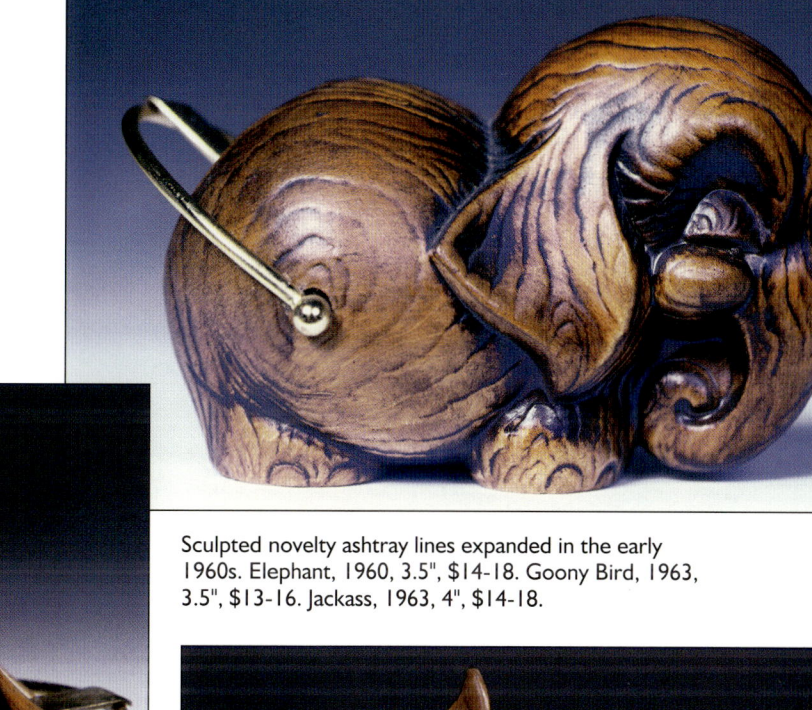

Sculpted novelty ashtray lines expanded in the early 1960s. Elephant, 1960, 3.5", $14-18. Goony Bird, 1963, 3.5", $13-16. Jackass, 1963, 4", $14-18.

Prospector log bank, 1960s, 3.5", $9-12.

The Promise of the 1960s 91

Salt and Pepper Sets

Roadrunner and Cactus shakers, 1960s, 4", $10-13.

The fun designs and intricate details of Treasure Craft novelties made them likely candidates for after market embellishment, such as the late '60s day-glo paint job given to this Ubangi shaker set on stand, 4.5". Unadulterated, $24-28.

Courting Frogs shakers on stand, factory painted, 1960s, 4.5", $10-13.

This sinister Skull and Keg set later found fans among Halloween collectors, 1960s, 3.75", $18-22.

92   The Promise of the 1960s

Cowboy and Cowgirl shakers, fashioned from the Hawaiian Tiki Tourist molds, 1960s, 5.5", $13-16.

Shaker sets of fish, flora, and fauna were sold in appropriate venues across North America in the 1960s and '70s, $9-12/ea. set.

The Promise of the 1960s   93

Souvenir Subsets

Las Vegas/Casinos

Las Vegas scenic tray featuring now rebuilt or defunct casinos, c. 1960s, 7.75", $15-20.

Scalloped Vegas dice tray, c. 1970, 8", $12-15.

94 The Promise of the 1960s

Double footprint tray,
c. 1970, 8.5", $18-20.

Las Vegas casino tray showing c. 1970 avocado glaze, 12.25", $18-24.

The Promise of the 1960s   95

Floridiana

Floridiana by Treasure Craft included standard nameplate items, Disneyana, and special lines specific to the Sunshine State. A few examples: Butterfly fish ashtray, c. 1965, 6.5", $10-14; Flamingo mug, c. 1970, 5.5", $8-12; Alligator tray, c. 1965, 8", $18-20; State scenes tray with Space Center, 7.75", c. 1970, $15-18.

The 1970s: A Decade of Change

Treasure Craft started the 1970s offering its widest variety ever. Homes across North America boasted their wood stained canister sets, serving trays, and figurines. Country styles appealed to traditional decorators, while vivid, swirling colors and abstract leaf shapes found favor with urbanites. Kids snuck snacks from sculpted animal cookie jars, and international travelers took home Treasure Craft's Hawaiian dancers and souvenirs.

But huge changes were brewing, not only within Treasure Craft and the pottery industry, but in society at large. Time spent on home decorating and cleaning became scarce as homemakers joined the workforce, and the spread of microwaves and dishwashers necessitated hardier ware that required little care. Fewer people found time to save grocery stamps and redeem them at Treasure Craft's largest account, the S&H Green Stamps Redemption Centers, which soon faded into obscurity.

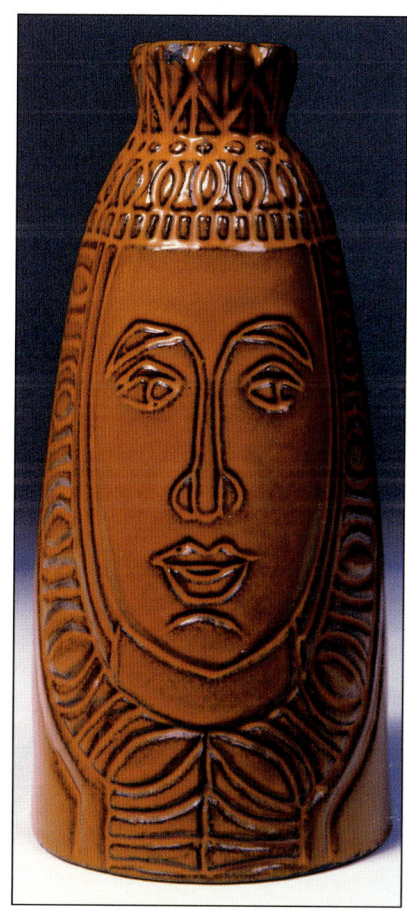

Face bottle vase, part of a line by stoneware muralist Raul Coronel, a family friend of the Levins known for creating large scale murals in Los Angeles, c. 1970, 9.75", $50-60.

Butterfly Line was a big seller in the ecology conscious early '70s. Canisters: Coffee and Tea, 7.5", $14-18/ea.; Sugar and Flour, 9.5", $15-20/ea.; Napkin or letter holder, 5.5", $12-15.

As social and labor strife swept the nation, the long-held notion that American wares were superior to less costly Japanese goods evaporated. Meanwhile, studio and home potters captured the imagination of giftware buyers. Brayton Laguna, whose wood tone ceramics enticed homemakers in the early 1950s, collapsed in 1968. While this eliminated a major competitor for Treasure Craft, it also portended doom for the state's major potteries, which had employed tens of thousands at their peak.

Viewed through this lens, Treasure Craft's ability to survive two energy crises, internal struggles, and 1970s economic stagnation was remarkable! New techniques derived from its Pottery Craft sibling propelled Treasure Craft through a decade in which most of its competitors failed.

Early '70s Experimentation

Wood stain was still popular, especially Treasure Craft's iconic Mushroom and Owl lines, with their psychedelic colors. The venerable Fruit and Barrel lines added the new 1970s kitchen colors of Honey, Persimmon, and Avocado, their lettering and other details highlighted in black. Many other lines of kitchenware were briefly decorated in these colors, including several of the leaf-shaped serving trays, a new stacking canister set, and a *Happy Face* line which included shakers, plaques, and a flask.

These alterations helped prolong the life of Treasure Craft's existing lines, but Levin foresaw the need for new designs and more durable wares. The retirement of longtime art director Tony Guerrero left a stylistic void, which Levin sought to fill with other artistic talent.

Los Angeles muralist Raul Coronel was finding fame around 1970 as an independent stoneware artist. Coronel created a now scarce line of abstract bottle vases for Treasure Craft, bearing elaborate "sun god" facial designs and decorated in the new solid color glazes. His designs were considered too radical for the mass market, and appeared in the line only briefly.

Happy Face flask in honey and walnut, c. 1970, 6.5", $15-20.

Elephant planter with whimsical, abstract features characteristic of early '70s pottery, 11" x 12", $25-29.

Frog planter, c. 1970, 4", $12-15.

Boy and girl wall pockets in early '70s colors, 6.5" and 7.5", $16-20/ea.

Concurrently, Levin sought the expertise of studio potter Robert Maxwell in developing a stoneware art line. While their short-lived *Stone Craft* alliance failed, the lessons learned would help set the stage for the *Pottery Craft* company, which would debut in 1973. (The full story is told in the Pottery Craft section of this book.)

The year 1971 saw a dramatic internal struggle at Treasure Craft. Faced with inflation and the specter of government wage and price controls, a new generation of factory workers sought to unionize the company. Used to a close-knit, hands-on style of operation, Levin was surprised and dismayed by the internal strife. Unionization was ultimately accepted, but its higher labor costs made Treasure Craft's elaborate hand-decorating techniques uncompetitive.

1971 also saw the genesis of an important twenty-five-year relationship with Disneyland and the new Disney World theme park. Treasure Craft had long produced souvenirs for attractions in all fifty states, and Disney commissioned a line of molded mugs and trays for sale at the parks. By agreement, all were marked "Walt Disney Productions", with second billing (or none at all) for Treasure Craft.

More important was Disney's agreement to sell a variety of standard Treasure Craft products at the parks. Florida pineapple trays, spoon rests, even the ponderous bull and matador sets would soon be packed around by eager tourists. More lines exclusive to the Disney parks also followed; offered at the March 24, 1972 opening of the Country Bear Jamboree were Treasure Craft banks and cookie jars in the visage of "Big Al", the bear band's guitarist.

98   The 1970s: A Decade of Change

Experimenting with a foam rubber stamping process developed at Pottery Craft, Cache Pots were colored with sputnik-style abstract plant designs. Though this labor-intensive process didn't last long, it would prove important in the development of Treasure Craft's popular 1980s southwestern styles.

Cache Pots met the surge in demand for indoor plants, available in the three standard pot sizes sold by nurseries in the early '70s. Faces: Small, $10-12; Medium, $12-15; Large, $15-20. Others: $5-7/ea.

Available only at the new *Country Bears Jamboree* attraction, Big Al was the first Disney character commissioned to Treasure Craft, 1972. Bank, 8.5", $29-35; Cookie jar (not shown), 11.5", $55-65.

New Designs, New Techniques

The end of 1972 heralded the extension of family involvement in the firm's management. Levin's son Bruce had worked at the plant and with his father at gift shows since childhood, but never intended to return after graduating from the University of California at Berkeley in 1969. Realizing the pressures facing Treasure Craft, the senior Levin asked Bruce back to the plant. "Initially, I was just going to help improve work flow on the factory floor," Bruce explained; but the need for stoneware led him to develop Pottery Craft as a separate operation across the street in Compton.

Pottery Craft's wild success defied the recession caused by the 1973 energy crisis, influencing the elder Levin to draw his son into management and product development decisions at Treasure Craft in 1974. Dressing up old lines with faddish colors would not solve the dilemma posed by the aging wood stain wares, which weren't dishwasher safe and required gentler handling. Bruce felt it was time to find other decorating techniques.

"My first attempt at underglaze decoration was the *Cache Pot* line. We'd learned from our success at Pottery Craft that people were starting to have lots of indoor plants, so we developed garden ware to fit the three main sizes of plastic nursery containers," Bruce related.

New to the firm in 1972, Bruce Levin brought Pottery Craft's foam rubber stamp glaze application to this Sputnik-like Cache Pot. The technique eventually led to Treasure Craft's successful 1980s Taos dinnerware. #453, 4.5", $10-12.

The 1970s: A Decade of Change

The Antique White Solution

Bruce Levin's first priority for Treasure Craft was to develop new techniques that could wear a hardy clear overglaze. A non-melting refractory brown pigment was rubbed over details on the white body, which then was sealed under a clear glaze. *Antique*, a slightly off-white base color, debuted in the 1975 Treasure Craft line. Dark wood cabinetry and furniture were cresting in popularity, and the white ware proved popular for its nice contrast—and its ability to withstand the dishwasher.

Antique was embellished in many ways. The yellow and rust glazes that decorated entire pieces in the early '70s now were used as accent colors under the glaze on the Antique pieces, and as detailing on some older wood stain lines.

A comparison of Antique wares with their identical wood stained twins shows that the appearance of some lines benefited from the new coloration, while others suffered. The logical conclusion was to create more lines suitable to Antique, and to use it in new ways. New decorations were tried, from impressed faces and floral patterns to embossed fruit in contrasting colors of yellows, browns, greens, and purples.

Don Winton and the Cookie Jar Sculptors

Antique found exciting new uses in the cookie jar line. First hired to design Treasure Craft cookie jars in the 1960s, Don Winton had become a close family friend. "Our Twin Winton company was priced out of our real estate in San Juan Capistrano, and we decided to sell out in 1977. I thought Treasure Craft was the logical choice to buy our molds," Don Winton noted. "I'd been sculpting for the Levins for years, so it seemed like a good fit, especially since we'd emulated their rubbed wood tones on our jars."

The Levins did buy Twin Winton's molds, honoring their originality and Winton's request by retiring and never reproducing them. Instead, Levin continued to commission Winton to sculpt new designs, or restyle old examples. The *Rocking Horse* and *Mouse Boy with Airplane* were among the first Winton designs to wear the new antique glaze, highlighted with yellows, greens, and browns.

Sculpted cookie jars and banks by Don Winton and other designers were important to Treasure Craft's survival in the 1970s. Farmer Pig bank by Winton is shown in the more desirable multi-color glazes on antique, c. 1975, 7.5", $22-26.

Many cookie jars were offered in both antique white and walnut/wood stain through the 1970s. Items not shown elsewhere: *Top row:* Cookie Chef, 12", $30-36; Milk Can, antique, $18-22; Milk Can, walnut, $15-18. *Middle row:* Teddy Bear Chief, Winton design, 12", $30-40; Bow Tie Bear, 10.5", $24-27; Juke Box, 10.5" (larger than 1992 version), $60-75. *Bottom row:* Ma's Cookie Books, 10", $24-29; Coffeepot, a sales leader designed by Scott Ferguson, 11.5", $19-24; Goose, 11", $22-25; Cookie Balloon, 11.5", $100-125.

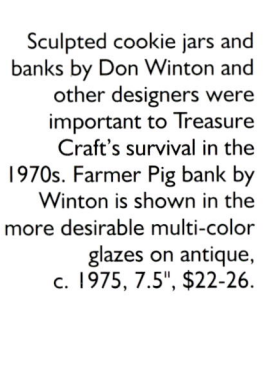

Rocking Horse cookie jar, Winton design, 12", $32-38.

Still a sculptor, Winton took a break from the bust he was crafting for the Smithsonian Air and Space Museum to elaborate. "My brother Ross and I were big Disney cartoon fans, so even our 1930s designs were based on their happy, round style of animation. I had great rapport with the Levins, so when I brought them ideas, I really emphasized large, expressive cartoon eyes…I thought their cookie jars needed more whimsy."

Winton would sculpt a dozen or more of Treasure Craft's most popular jars in the '70s, most offered in both wood stain and antique. Other hit cookie jars for the firm were free-lance designer Scott Ferguson's *Coffeepot, Tug Boat, Cookie Van,* and *Trolley Car*.

As Antique began to supplant wood stain, Treasure Craft saw the potential for other underglaze colors. A warm peach/beige tone was introduced in the late '70s on molds borrowed from the still separate Pottery Craft firm. Cast in earthenware as Treasure Craft's *Butterfly,* they became the company's first all-new line of kitchenware since the 1960s.

A pretty floral spray decal was applied to speckled white kitchenware, attracting distribution deals from J.C. Penney and other national department stores. *Poppy*, along with Butterfly, became the industry's first complete new lines of coordinated, decal-based housewares in years, and the first ever to use lithographed decals.

Mouse Boy cookie jar with Airplane by Winton, 12.5", $32-38. Bank (not shown), 7.5", $22-25.

Poppy tableware pattern dealer plaque, late 1970s, 4", $12-15.

Transferware Modernizes Production

Antique offered Treasure Craft the opportunity to experiment with decal decorating. Heat resistant transfer decals could be permanently fired into the clear overglaze. "Hand decorating was getting to be too costly, and we needed something that could take decals so we could offer more designs," Bruce Levin clarified.

The pottery sourced lithographic decals from Europe. Realistic flora and fauna decals matched late '70s preferences for literal, naturalistic themes. Souvenir ware began to sprout owls, and butterflies of different species appeared. By decade's end, silkscreen decals of everything from sailboats to birds appeared in decal form on Treasure Craft giftware.

Antique's advantage was that transfers could be fired under the glaze, making any number of dishwasher and oven safe patterns possible.
Butterfly on crackle bottle vase, c. 1980, 6", $10-12.

The 1970s: A Decade of Change

These patterns proved a success in the earth tone crazy 1970s, and matched accent colors on Treasure Craft's cookie jars, planters, and other sculpted ware. Inspired by southwest tribal pottery, the most elegant treatment of these earth tones was on the late '70s *Pueblo Collection*. Stylized birds and deeply geometric patterns in glazed antique or exposed natural underglaze colors were crowned by pigmented turquoise jewels. Introduced as a small line of planters and bath accessories, Pueblo proved predictive of 1980s design trends, and would help lead Treasure Craft to its greatest success as the new decade dawned.

By 1979, Treasure Craft had reinvented itself. New designs and processes found the firm large new accounts. But high inflation and energy shortages precipitated by the Iran Hostage Crisis promised an uncertain future for Treasure Craft and the few remaining large California potters.

Pueblo Collection introduced Treasure Craft's unglazed Natural background colors in the late '70s. *Top row:* Large tapered pot, #153, 10.5", $28-32; Bulbous vase, #152, 10.5", $18-20; Wedding vase, #155, 12", $28-32; Cookie jar with bear lid, 14.5", $55-65. *Middle row:* Bud vase, #154, 8", $14-17; Arrowhead pot, large, #167, 8.5", $24-27; Low pot, medium, #166, 4.75", $18-22; Low pot, small, #165, 4.5", $12-15. *Bottom row:* Wide mouth pot, #168, 9", $24-27; Small tapered pot, #150, 4.5", $12-15; Bear pot, #151, 7.5", $18-20; Small flared pot, #156, 4.5", $12-15.

1970s Symbols

Happy Face plaque, c. 1970, 7.75", $14-18.

Happy Face shakers in avocado (also known in yellow), c. 1970, 4", $15-20/set.

Pueblo Line anticipated southwest decorating styles that would sweep America in the late '80s. #166 low pot, medium, antique, 4.75", $15-20.

102   The 1970s: A Decade of Change

Owl and Mushroom Lines, two definitive early '70s icons. *Owls:* Professor Owl full-bodied cookie jar, $25-30; Spoon rest/plaque, 9", $8-12; Shakers (two sizes), $6-9/set. *Mushrooms:* Canisters, set of three sizes, Lime, $35-40/set; Yellow-Orange, $40-45/set. Shakers: Lime, $8-10/pr.; Yellow-Orange, $12-16/pr.

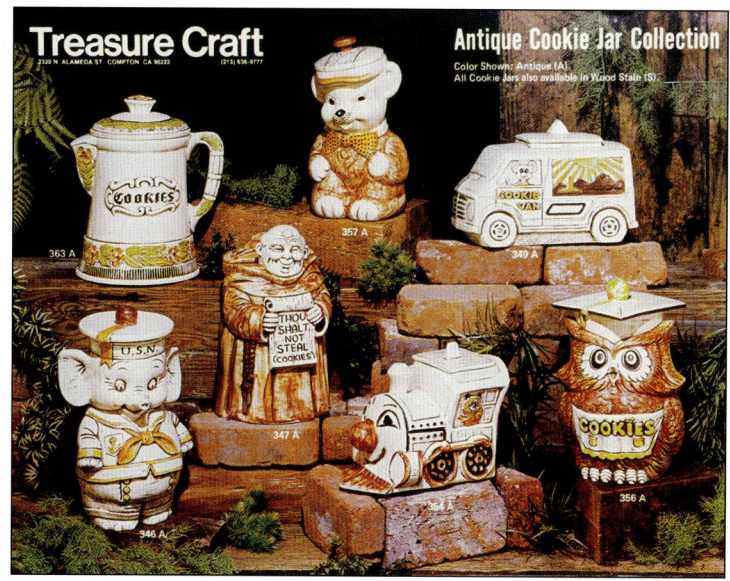

Cookie Jars and Canisters

Cookie Jar sales slick for new antique white glaze, 1975. *Top row:* Coffeepot jar by Ferguson, 11.5", $18-20; Beret bear, 11", $24-28; Cookie Van recalls mid-'70s van craze, 9", $60-70. *Bottom row:* Sailor Elephant, 11.5", Shown: $32-40, Multicolor (not shown): $60-70; Monk by Don Winton, 11", $20-25; Locomotive, 9", $29-34; Professor Owl, novelty version, 11.5", $24-26.

Treasure Craft decorators started using different 1960s glaze colors together on Butterfly pieces like this syrup pitcher, c. 1970, 5.75", $24-27.

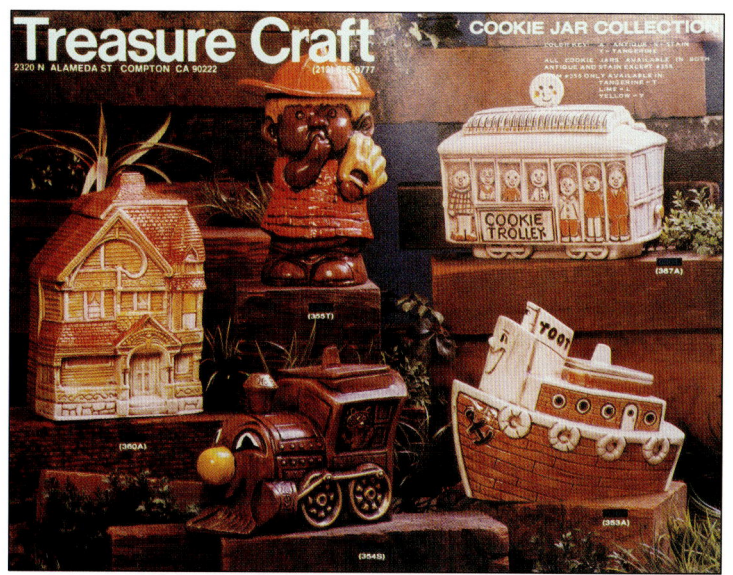

A late '70s cookie jar slick shows that some jars still fared better in the old wood stain finish. Victorian House, 12", $25-30; Baseball boy had multi-ethnic appeal in the '70s, 10.5", $30-36; Cookie Trolley, 9", $30-35; Locomotive, 9", $35-40; Tugboat, 10", $60-70.

Attractive use of Red on this 5" mug, c. 1970, $11-15.

The 1970s: A Decade of Change

Ice Wagon cookie jar, c. 1975, 11.5", $40-45.

Boy and girl canisters, c. 1970, 9.5", $14-16/ea. (Not shown: Sugar and Tea, 8.5", $12-14/ea.)

'70s Color Experiments

Potato Vine leaf pu pu dish, a 1960s Hawaiian inspiration coated in Honey glaze, c. 1970, $8-10.

Bandito represented a time when antiheroes were heroes, c. 1975, 11.5", $30-35.

Novelty Planters ad slick, c. 1975. *Top row:* Frog, 9", $24-28; Snail, 16", $28-32; Snail, 10.5", $24-28; Lioness, 10", $18-22. *Middle row:* Lion, 8", $18-22; Turtle, 7", $14-18; Hippo, 7", $24-28. *Small items:* 4"-5.5", $9-14.

104   The 1970s: A Decade of Change

Pottery Craft and the Stoneware Lines

A dwindling number of American ceramic firms confronted a new nemesis as the 1970s dawned. The budding studio movement and counter-cultural norms inspired a generation of "do-it-yourself" home potters, and ceramics courses for artists and amateurs became staples at colleges across America. Even as interest in pottery reached fever pitch, demand for the wares of traditional major potteries slumped.

Al Levin recognized that part of the appeal of the studio potters was the heft and durability of their stoneware lines. A new generation sought to get closer to nature, and prized handcrafted wares over rows of identically mass-produced items. Stoneware expressed quality and individuality, since no two pieces ever fired exactly alike.

High temperature stoneware production was technically difficult, quite different from the low-fired earthenware Treasure Craft had always produced. As he'd done in hiring Lee Shank to set up his first factory, Levin sought outside expertise to design and formulate stoneware.

Robert Maxwell and Stone Craft

Ceramic schools all over Southern California promoted stoneware development around 1960, and UCLA graduate Robert Maxwell brought it to national prominence as an art form in a 1961 show at the New York Museum of Modern Art. Maxwell then opened a studio across the street from Charles Eames in Venice, California; by the mid-1960s, it turned out small bottle vases, molded animal sculptures and a fun line of abstract "beasties" with gaping mouths and startled eyes.

Boutiques started to carry his stoneware creations, and with orders from San Francisco's opulent Gumps department store, production soared to over 15,000 units. Al Levin noted his success with interest, inviting him to form an alliance at the Compton plant in 1970.

"My motivation was to move from Venice and become a bigger producer," Maxwell says of his association with Treasure Craft. "My involvement was to develop a separate subsidiary called Stone Craft. I would build the high-fire reduction kilns needed for stoneware, create proper clay and glaze formulas, and design the line."

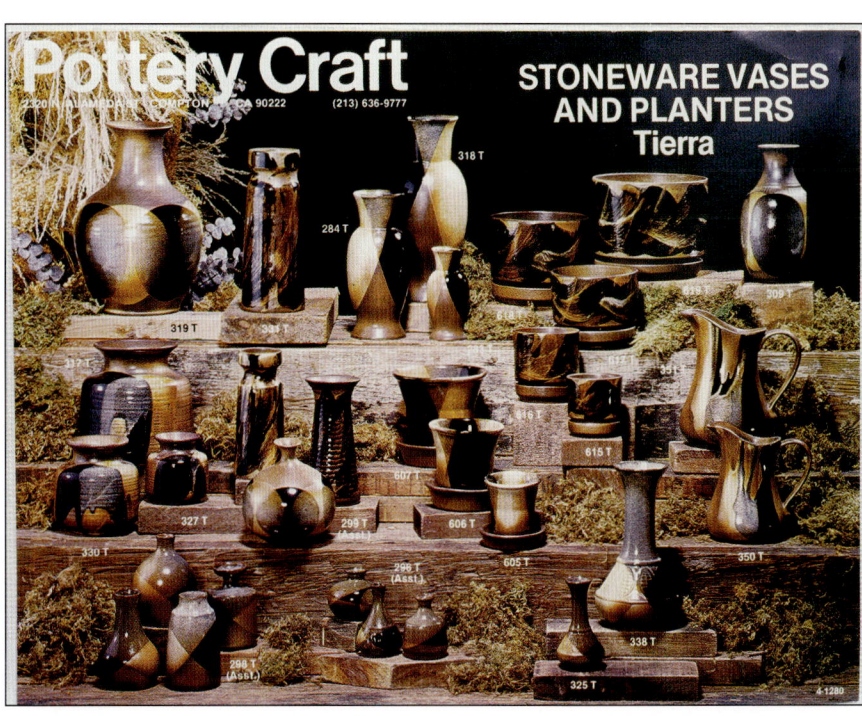

Pottery Craft's Bruce Levin merged modernist art pottery decorating techniques with production stoneware manufacturing in 1973. Moonstone color combination with desirable overlapping glazes, *top row*: Floor vase, #292, 11.5", $24-30; Wide vase, drip glaze, #127, 9.5", $28-32; Decanter and four slant top tumblers, #202, 9.5" and 3", $50-60/set; Floor vase, Maxwell design, #319, 16", $45-55. *Bottom row*: Assorted small vases: bottle vase and square shouldered vase, Maxwell, $25-30, others, $12-15; Ashtrays, stacking set of three, $18-22/set; Lighter and ashtray, $20-25/set.

Studio stoneware artist Robert Maxwell's brief tenure with the Compton plant in 1970 showed the way to overlapping glaze effects. Maxwell shaped certain designs shown here in Tierra colors, *from top left*: Floor vase, #319, $45-55; Stout vases, #317-330, $18-35; Bottle vase (only), #299, $28-32; Assorted vases, #298, $18-28. (Deduct for brush stroked glazes.)

Maxwell produced master molds for lines of vases and garden ware, ashtrays and animal sculptures, but left the Compton plant before stoneware production could ensue. While no one wanted to discuss the circumstances, all sides agreed the arrangement proved brief and unpleasant. In the end, Levin bought out Maxwell's molds and other interests for $16,000. Maxwell opened a new studio in Fallbrook, California, and Treasure Craft shelved the idea of stoneware production.

Eighteen months later, the need for something new seemed even more acute. Portland, Oregon's, Pacific Stoneware had achieved a line of heavily glazed kitchenware with funky designs that offered the look of hand-hewn studio pieces, while masking the uneven, unpredictable results of stoneware firing. Yet most major stores perceived stoneware as a gritty, clunky medium, with designs too idiosyncratic for the mass market. Treasure Craft understood it would take stylish design, smooth finishes, simple and modernistic glazes to reach a new, upscale stoneware buyer.

Maxwell's successful 1960 showing at the New York Museum of Modern Art led him to open a studio adjacent to Charles Eames in Venice, California. Pottery Craft vase, Maxwell design, 5", $24-28.

Bruce Levin and the Stoneware Experiments

But how could such a ware be perfected? The answer came courtesy of the collapse of the California real estate market in 1972. Levin's son Bruce was a fledgling architect who found himself part of an office-wide layoff. Instead of accepting a transfer, Bruce offered to temporarily return to help troubleshoot problems at Treasure Craft.

"I always intended to go back to architecture, but there's an old saying in pottery circles—once clay gets under your fingernails, it's hard to get rid of it!" laughed Bruce Levin about his introduction to stoneware production. "Dad asked me to help figure out how we could revamp the horns on the bulls so they wouldn't break, and I never ran out of things to do after that."

Working in the plant turned out to be a life changing experience, and Bruce became ingrained in the world of ceramic production. Late in 1972, he turned his attention to the question of stoneware. Though untrained as a ceramics engineer, he experimented with found materials and converted one of Treasure Craft's idle oxidation kilns into a high-fire reduction furnace.

"High-fire kilns were volatile, since they were dampered so the hot, unburned gas wouldn't escape…instead, it sought the iron oxide (oxygen) within the clays and glazes to complete its burn cycle," explained Bruce. In doing so, the resultant colors changed dramatically, so no two pieces were exactly alike. The resulting product fired at 2400 degrees Fahrenheit, producing a denser, heavier ware, with different textures and colors than Treasure Craft's low-fired earthenware. Importantly, his kilnsmen readily mastered the art of maintaining even cooking temperatures in the kiln so the glazes would vitrify.

Early pieces were quite crude, since Bruce added raw iron oxide to redden the clay. He soon changed the formula, using a red clay with natural iron oxide, firing it to a grey stoneware bisque. This proved just granular enough to take glaze colors easily, without the abrasive feel of its competitors.

Pottery Craft surprised major stores, who had presumed it impossible to sell stoneware art, gift, and kitchen pottery in volume. Decanter set, c. 1975, 9.5" and 3", $15-20.

Pottery Craft
PALOMINO

Palomino color combination, including naturalistic embossed and foam stamped designs. *Top row:* Floor vase, #293, 11.5", $30-35; Pitcher and bowl set, large, #355, $25-28; Embossed planter, #154, $14-18. *Middle row:* Medium vases, 8", $14-18/ea.; Small vases, #297: bottle and square shouldered, Maxwell molds, 4.5-5.5", $18-20; others, $9-14. *Bottom row:* Stacking ashtrays, #391-393, $7-10/set; Pitcher and bowl, small, #353, $12-16/set; Ashtray, #401, $7-10.

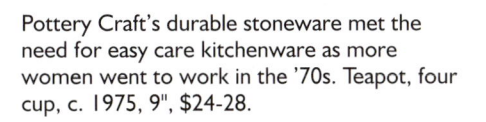

Pottery Craft's durable stoneware met the need for easy care kitchenware as more women went to work in the '70s. Teapot, four cup, c. 1975, 9", $24-28.

Textured planter, c. 1975, 9", $19-24.

Stylized cat figurine, c. 1975, 5.75" x 7.75", $24-28.

Pottery Craft and the Stoneware Lines   107

A Modern New Entity

Sensing promise, Bruce became founder and owner of Pottery Craft, opening a separate factory across the street from Treasure Craft. Experimenting with various glazes, the pieces were rubbed first with a refractory brown stain that wouldn't burn in the kiln, then hand-painted with highlights. Dipped geometric two-toned and drip glazes reminiscent of Maxwell's 1970 ideas were applied, then fired in the kiln to produce a the multi-color combinations of *Moonstone* (blue and white) and a black and tan combination known as *Tierra*. A clear overglaze created sheen and made it remarkably smooth to the touch. Also created was *Palomino*, its earthy base color accented with brown iron oxide patterns, which were applied with foam rubber stamps.

Creating a line of large planters and functional artware, Bruce joined his father at the January 1973 Atlantic City China and Glass Show. A radical departure from Treasure Craft's novelty lines, the Pottery Craft display was a standout, yet a scant $200 was sold. Results were similarly disappointing at the next week's Chicago Housewares Show. "Our big accounts didn't think they could sell high-fired artware in enough volume to stock," Bruce explained. Most department store buyers saw stoneware as the province of boutique studios, which were better positioned to sell lines that weren't uniform in appearance.

But the following week's show in Los Angeles proved to be the watershed for Pottery Craft. Familiar with studio stoneware, orders flooded in from California buyers anxious for a premium product at a production price. Customers who found stoneware novelties too funky welcomed Pottery Craft's sleek and sophisticated designs, and sales boomed. National accounts quickly followed the trend, and stoneware became an important part of the Compton output; Pottery Craft would ultimately lead Treasure Craft to a new era of style and design.

Stylish slant-top decanter set in Palomino, $30-35/set.

Tea set, c. 1975, $24-28/set.

A Full Line of Contemporary Tableware

Along with some of the Maxwell vase and ashtray molds, Pottery Craft introduced pitchers, garden ware, and large vases that had the appearance of wheel thrown pots. Masa Fujii became Pottery Craft's chief designer, shaping everything from cocktail sets with slant-top tumblers to canisters and casseroles. Pottery Craft invented new products in the mid-'70s, best evidenced by Bruce Levin's *Matsu Sprouter* created for home growers of the newly popular bean sprout. (Ironically, Pottery Craft was the first Compton line to use pieces made outside America, as the bamboo teapot handles could only be procured from Japan.)

By 1978, Pottery Craft offered a full line of kitchenware, and sales soared. Molds became ever more detailed, some wearing textured faces, others bearing embossed leaf designs. Geometric patterns applied with foam rubber stamps, brush stroked glazes, and the *Botanical* collection of naturalistic intaglio floral designs testified to the increasing skill of Pottery Craft decorators and designers.

Bruce Levin begin to share direction of the Treasure Craft operations with his father in the mid-'70s. Though the two firms continued to operate separately, Pottery Craft's new shapes and designs began to extend to its larger sibling. An important addition was a bowl jiggering machine from Germany, making Compton one of very few potteries that could make smooth sided canisters and planters in high volume.

Matsu Sprouter designed by Bruce Levin, late 1970s, 7.5", $19-25.

Figural Whimsies

Conversely, Treasure Craft's heritage of fun, novel figurines influenced Bruce to create whimsies in stoneware. *The Clay Menagerie*, an extensive line of whimsical stoneware animals, captivated giftware buyers on its appearance in 1975. Designer Mitsuo utilized Pottery Craft's unglazed grey stoneware, adding glaze-painted details. The animals wore string tags introducing them by name, including *Igor Beaver*, *Dr. Wisequack*, *Romeow* the Cheshire Cat, *Sluggo Snail,* and *Maxie Mouse*. Larger figurines were followed by a smaller line, gift boxed in a way reminiscent of 1949's Treasure Craft Sprites. Within a few years, Clay Menagerie characters adorned small dresser or desk trays as well.

Romeow of the Clay Menagerie, late 1970s, 3.75", $14-18 with name tag.

New jiggering machines made high volume production of this #470 canister possible in the late '70s, 9.5", $10-12.

Pottery Craft's high-temperature reduction furnaces could also cook porcelain bisque wares like this Don Winton designed owls on log figure, late '70s, 8", $14-18.

Pottery Craft and the Stoneware Lines

The success of Clay Menagerie spurred further experimentation at Pottery Craft in 1978. Responding to a craze generated by the book *Gnomes*, Don Winton designed the translucent *Forest Folk* line of figurines. A translucent porcelain bisque which could fire at the same temperature as stoneware was the base material, and minor, hand-painted embellishments could be added by the decorators at will. Pottery Craft extended the short-lived porcelain technique into a series of Winton designed cats and holiday ornaments featuring angels and mice.

But Pottery Craft's biggest success may arguably have been one of its last lines. *South of the Border* featured a large sombrero chip-and-dip, shakers, and a cookie jar featuring a Latino at siesta, and other southwest style designs. Treasure Craft merged with Pottery Craft, using many of these molds as blanks for *Taos* and other southwest style dinner and tableware that would lead the firm to its zenith.

Pottery Craft lamp, stored at the factory since the late '70s. Very few of these prototypes were produced, 30". Rare. Value unknown.

The large scale of certain Pottery Craft vases and planters made them attractive candidates to be used as lamp bases. A handful of prototypes were wired, with handsome results, but Pottery Craft had few accounts in the home furnishing field. The expense of adding electrical components and weak demand during the energy crisis stifled efforts to put them into the line, and only a few are known to have ever left the plant.

'70s Shapes Lead '80s Styling

By the 1980s, the stoneware craze began to abate, as a shift away from earth tones in home decor took hold. Pottery Craft extended its life by adding transfer decals, such as the *Farm Fresh* kitchenware designed by Rodger Johnson of the Center for Houseware Designs. These hearty looking pie plates and cookware matched tin and wooden kitchen accessories offered by other housewares firms, and were the first Compton product packaged for sale in wooden crates.

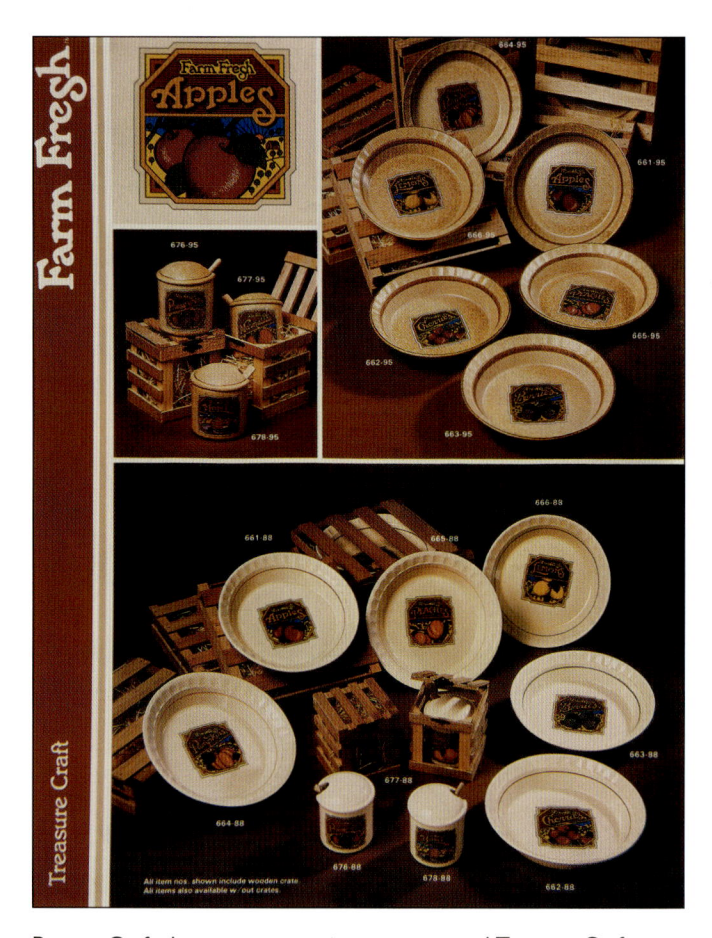

Pottery Craft shapes were cast in stoneware and Treasure Craft earthenware for Rodger Johnson's Farm Fresh design, first to be sold in crates, c. 1980. Pie or quiche bakers, crated, 11.5": Stoneware, $18-24/ea.; Earthenware, $15-20/ea. Condiments with lids and spoons, crated, 6": Stoneware, $13-18/ea.; Earthenware, $10-15/ea.

In the last few years of stoneware production, several molds were cross-pollinated in this way. The molds were not changed, which has caused confusion in collectors who see Pottery Craft marks on earthenware Taos siesta spoon rests, or find Don Winton's monk cookie jar cast in stoneware—but with a Treasure Craft mark. A few transitional pieces even bore both names, until Treasure Craft eliminated stoneware production and merged the firms in 1985.

South of the Border

Treasure Craft

Pottery Craft's South of the Border collection was the genesis of the Taos dinnerware service that swelled Treasure Craft's fortunes in the 1980s. *Top photo:* Cookie jar, siesta, 11", $30-35; Sombrero chip and dip, 12", $24-28; Siesta shakers, 4.5", $14-18; Straw hat serving bowl, 9", $15-20. *Bottom photo:* Footed mug, 4", $9-12; Other mugs, 3"-5", $4-6/ea.; Ashtrays: $4-6/ea.

Only recently has stoneware begun to be appreciated for its place in the development of modern pottery. Seminal designers like Maxwell have begun to be profiled in histories of California pottery, and a Pottery Craft vase glazed in Tierra's black and tan overlapping circles appeared in the iconic decor of television's *That 70s Show*. The kitchenware blanks were timeless enough that some would still be in use a quarter-century hence.

The quality and style embodied by Pottery Craft's hardy wares testifies to the ingenuity of their creators and producers.

Pottery Craft Kitchenware

Remember when people were "foxy?" So '70s mug, 3", $6-8.

Botanica carafe in Tierra, late 1970s, 11", $28-32.

Treasure Craft's Monk cookie jar by Don Winton, cast in Pottery Craft stoneware, c. 1980, $25-29.

Pottery Craft and the Stoneware Lines

Pottery Craft hang tags explained stoneware process, written to suit the "earthy and free" '70s ethos.

This Stoneware Original was created by Pottery Craft's most accomplished and imaginative artisans. Combining the basic elements of earth, fire, and water, it was hand-decorated and high fired to a temperature approaching 2400°F. This process enables Pottery Craft to express the earthy nature of the ceramic arts. Each work of art is a unique, original creation.

In keeping with a traditional art form established in China during the Sung Dynasty, 960 A.D. - 1223 A.D., Pottery Craft explores in a free and inventive way the liveliness of form and the spirited use of color, texture, and decoration.

This is Stoneware at its very best. Decorative and useful, it is food and dishwasher-safe...designed to bring you long-lasting pleasure.

A complete line of kitchen and serving ware was offered in Palomino in this sales sheet, c. 1980. Items not shown elsewhere:
- Baker, #873, $15-20.
- Bowl, lug, #868, $4-6.
- Bowls, mixing, set of three, #975, $42-50/set.
- Canisters, set of four, #965, $40-50/set.
- Canister, cookies, #960, $12-15.
- Casserole/lid, #985, $15-20.
- Cheese shaker, #906, $6-8.
- Creamer, #968, $4-6.
- Crock/ladle, #982, $18-20.
- Honey jar/spinner, #380, $12-16.
- Jar/bale, three sizes, $8-12/ea.
- Mug, #833, $4-6.
- Pitcher, milk, #977, $10-14.
- Quiche pan, #878, $14-18.
- Relish tray, five parts, #533, $20-25.
- Shakers, #967, $4-6.
- Spoon rest, #971, $4-6.
- Sugar/lid, #968, $5-7.
- Teapot, #831, $22-26.
- Trivet, #874, $7-10.
- Tureen with ladle, #981, $24-28.

Vases and Planters

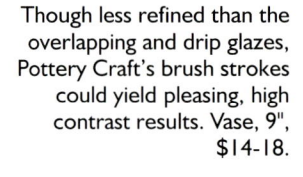

Though less refined than the overlapping and drip glazes, Pottery Craft's brush strokes could yield pleasing, high contrast results. Vase, 9", $14-18.

Hanging planter in overlapping Moonstone coloration, #486, c. 1975, 8.5", $18-24.

112   Pottery Craft and the Stoneware Lines

Pottery Craft stoneware lent itself to designs inspired by the pottery of indigenous cultures. All sides of this planter/bowl bore different sculpted faces and figures, #210, c. 1975, 9.75", $22-28.

Country Collectibles embossed kitchenware in Palomino and Cinnamon on white, c. 1980.
  Canisters, set of four, #520, $40-48/set.
  Cookie, #509, $15-18.
  Creamer, #521, $5-7.
  Pitcher, pint, #511, $9-11.
  Pitcher, 2 qts., #510, $18-22.
  Shakers, #522, $4-6.
  Spice jars, #650, $5-7/ea.
  Sugar/lid, #521, $6-8.
  Utensil caddy, #492, $12-15.

Later Stoneware Colors

Jade Collection, late '70s. Few pieces of this briefly produced color scheme have reached the collector market, so pricing information is as yet uncertain.

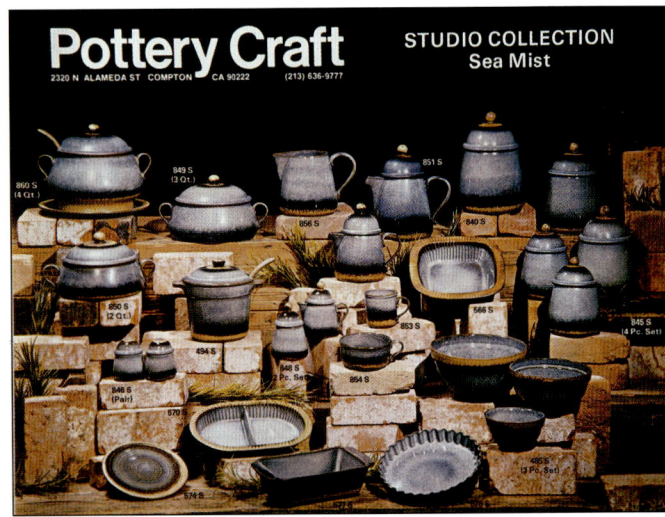

Sea Mist, an attractive grey-blue or greenish glaze offered exclusively through J.C. Penney, c. 1980. Too few pieces have surfaced for current values to be known.

Porcelain Figurines

A Forest Folk gnome stands with Mouse ornaments, c. 1980, 2.75"-4". Gnome, $12-14; Mice, $7-9/ea.

Porcelain bisque holiday decorations were a Pottery Craft sideline, c. 1980. Ornaments, 1.75-4.25", $6-9/ea.; Bells, 5.5-6.5", $8-14/ea.; Dealer plaque, 4", $12-16/ea.

Porcelain animals, c. 1980, 3"-6". Spaniel, #5521, $15-18; Cats, assorted, $12-15/ea.; Bunny #5531, $12-15. (Prices do not include optional stands.)

Turtle Lou, 2.75", $12-15.

Clay Menagerie

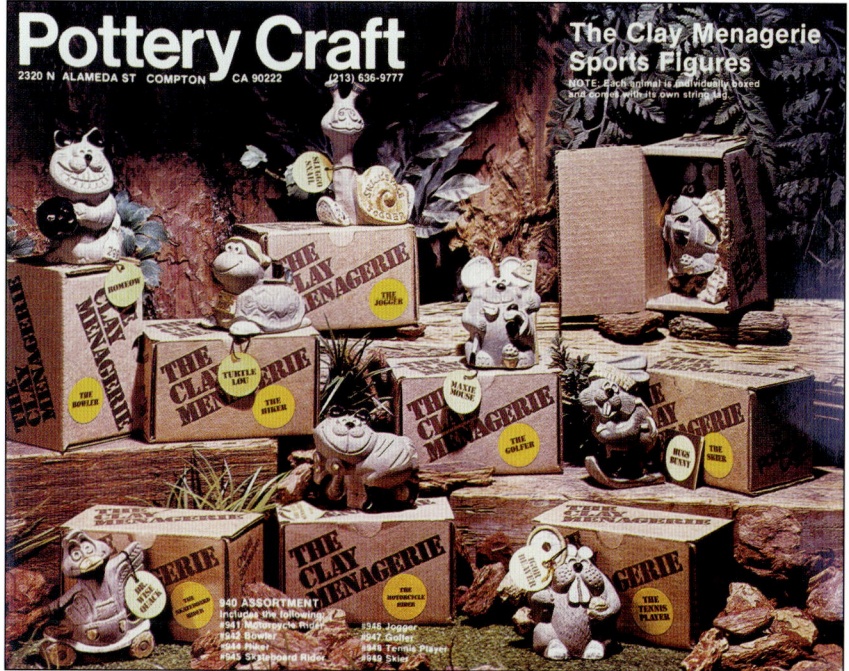

Sophisti-Cat, c. 1980. Small, 2.5", $12-15; Large, 3.5", $14-17.

Clay Menagerie Sports Figures, shown with original tags and boxes, late 1970s, 3.75"-5", $16-22/ea.

Pottery Craft and the Stoneware Lines 115

Three renditions of Ram Bunctious. Small figure, 2.75", $12-15; Tray, 6.25", $16-20; Large figure, 3", $15-18.

Maxie Mouse, 2.5", $14-16.

Greetings line of Dr. Wisequack paperweights, 5". (Note early application of Treasure Craft earthenware nameplate to Mt. Rainier version.) $15-20/ea.

Greetings desk accessory showing Clay Menagerie hang tag, 5", $15-20.

Igor Beaver, 3.5", $14-18.

116 Pottery Craft and the Stoneware Lines

Big Successes in the Big '80s

"Sometimes you survive, sometimes you thrive." This maxim described how the 1980s evolved, both for Treasure Craft and American industry in general.

A second energy crisis and record inflation raged in 1980. Kilns were expensive to run, and customers hard-pressed to buy. The tattered California pottery industry would soon lose most of its remaining players, including giant dinnerware marker Franciscan, which moved to England in 1984.

Yet Treasure Craft survived, and ultimately thrived. The difficult lessons of the early '80s spurred the firm to its greatest successes, and by decade's end, Treasure Craft had become California's last major producer of ceramic gift housewares.

It helped that the Compton factory started the 1980s with two successful kitchenware lines, Poppy and Butterfly. Transfers sealed onto speckled antique white and peachy beige blanks covered everything from bath sets to kitchen and serving pieces. Their mellow, attractive colors and detailed decals made them pillars of J.C. Penney's home fashions department.

Treasure Craft grew to be California's last major pottery on the success of its 1980s southwest styles. Many of the molds drew from Pottery Craft designs, including vase shapes created by Robert Maxwell in 1970. Double handled vase #167 and Maxwell shape #122, $28-32. Large vases and planter (#136, #166, #134, #122, #165), $20-30/ea. Maxwell molds, #123 and 124, $18-24/ea. Smaller vases and planter (#164, #135, #121), $12-18/ea.

Chinese Birds crackle vase, c. 1980, 7.75", $24-28.

Survival and growth required improved machinery, which came with the 1982 purchase of the equipment of California Originals, the Torrance pottery which had emulated Treasure Craft's wood stained cookie jars and variegated glaze tableware over two decades. Contrary to popular belief, Treasure Craft did not purchase the defunct company's outdated molds, as their Cal Style cookie jars were too vaguely detailed and required costly poured castings and rubbed finishes.

Poppy and Butterfly were Treasure Craft's first complete lines of coordinated kitchen and dinnerware, c. 1980. (Complete listings and prices of dinnerware in tables to follow.)

New Design Influences

Instead, Treasure Craft created its own crisp new designs, combining the venerable white crackle glaze with elegant new transfer designs of *Chinese Birds* and *Dogwood* on a host of vases, hurricane candles, and decorative accessories. Their Oriental flavor was a formal departure from Treasure Craft's predominately casual designs.

For the country decorator, a transferware revival of Victorian pitcher-and-bowl washstand sets and accessories was designed. Vibrant floral sprays and *Harvest Wheat* stalks contrasted with white glazed earthenware, meant to simulate ironstone. Though the fad faded quickly, they were a needed success during the early '80s recession.

The 1982 recession and import issues canceled plans to open a Treasure Craft of Canada subsidiary, and Treasure Craft of Hawaii was nearing the end of its quarter-century of production. To eliminate duplication of effort, Pottery Craft merged into Treasure Craft by the mid-'80s. Lacking these long-time sources of design inspiration, Treasure Craft looked outside, producing licensed characters for the first time.

Based on David Kirschner's *Rose Petal Place* characters, a new line of cookie jars debuted in 1983. These sculpted jars had to be precisely detailed and hand-painted to match their television counterparts. Coach P. D. Centipede's football hut demonstrated a new level of skill in glaze formulation and firing techniques, skills Treasure Craft quickly applied to all of the company's jars.

Dogwood transferware accessories led Treasure Craft's transition to pastels in the early 1980s. *Top row:* Vase, #284, $15-20; Hurricane candle, #172, $25-30; Floor vase, #319, $27-30; Floor vase, #292, $24-28; Pitcher and washstand bowl, #255, $30-34; Small vases, #298, $10-15; Lighter, #62, $12-18; Ashtrays: Large, #98, $6-8; Small, #97, $4-6.

As a result, the old wood staining technique was discontinued in 1984. Pastels, jewel tones, and graceful geometric shapes based on style revivals from the 1930s, '40s, and '50s were now in vogue, and Treasure Craft sought to capture this neo-deco feeling in a line of *Fashion Vases*. Offered in gloss and matte colors, this wide line was characterized by graceful, swooping lines and architectural proportions.

Transferring over from Pottery Craft, designers Masa Fujii and Masami "Mami" Kato followed with their signature *Masa Mami* line in 1984. Mold shop manager Jon Bassi tooled separate collars for vases and vessels, fused to contrasting bodies to create two-toning in pastels. Rivaling 1980s studio pottery, Masa Mami was sophisticated and artistic, its smooth geometry often broken by exaggerated, sharp lines and texturing. It was also a sales flop. Bruce Levin shook his head as he explained, "We thought it was beautifully styled, but our big store accounts decided it was over the heads of their customers, so they wouldn't buy."

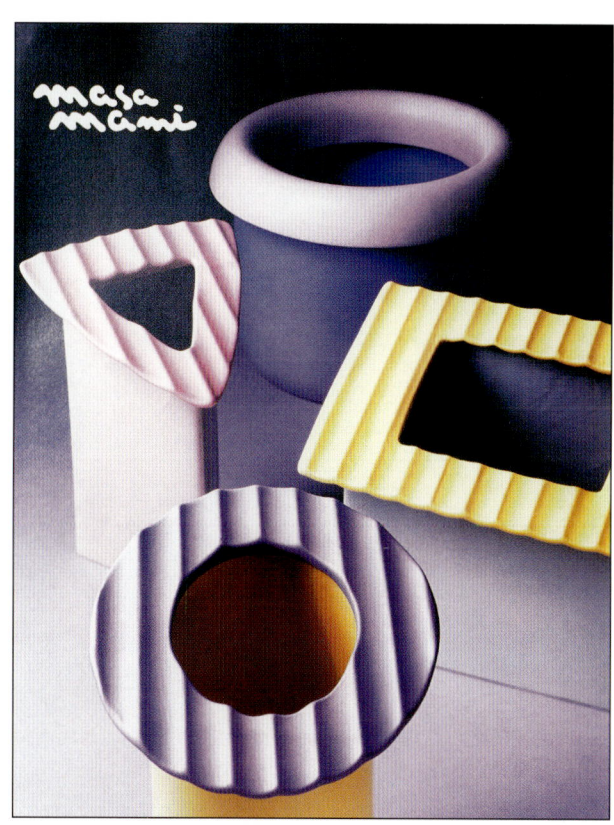

Masa Mami designer vases, early 1980s. Textured geometric collars, $28-35/ea. Rolled collar planter, $18-24.

Big Successes in the Big 80's 119

Southwestern Styles

By 1984, the mantel of managerial control had passed to Bruce from his father, who reached a state of semi-retirement. It was a pivotal year for Treasure Craft, as the younger Levin took the firm in new directions.

The first was a revival of the foam stamp decorating technique Bruce had experimented with in the early '70s. Utilizing the South of the Border molds Bruce had developed for Pottery Craft, a new pattern featuring chili pepper and geometric desert dweller motifs on a white earthenware base was born.

Al and Jeanette Levin around the time of his retirement from day-to-day management at Treasure Craft.

Big Successes in the Big 80's

Taos was introduced as a limited set of canisters and kitchen accessories, but the appealing design of chalky, hand-applied colors was an instant hit. Levin had correctly anticipated the trend towards southwest style decor that would sweep America in the latter part of the '80s, and a barrage of new pieces appeared. Line mates came quickly, as the popular *Southwest* vase line was matched with transferware featuring Navajo rug geometric forms on natural colored blanks.

By the mid-'80s, Treasure Craft offered several variations of southwestern designs. Their popularity caught the notice of buyers for Mervyn's department stores, a chain that was growing dramatically along the west coast. They contacted Treasure Craft to design a dinnerware line proprietary to them.

In its four decades of production, Treasure Craft had never made basic place settings of plates, cups, and bowls to match its kitchenware lines. Its equipment was not easily adapted to cost-effectively form these pieces, but when rival J.C. Penney also demanded place settings to match Poppy, Taos, and Butterfly, Treasure Craft responded. Jiggering and ram pressing machines now worked alongside the traditional slip cast molds.

Mirage was the name given to the new line for Mervyn's. Debuting as a complete dinnerware service, it was decorated with a simple pink to blue-green band on creamy white. Though it appeared brush stroked, close inspection revealed that the band was a densely printed transfer under the glaze; only the darker lines enfolding it were painted by hand.

Treasure Craft's new place settings enhanced the firm's burgeoning quality reputation, their heft due in part to the thickness required by their old-fashioned production processes. But trouble presented itself when Mirage sales vastly eclipsed expectations, outstripping the pottery's ability to fill orders. To meet demand, Treasure Craft licensed certain pieces in Mirage and Southwest to be made in Japan, making additional place settings available while Levin scrambled to add capacity.

Creative styling and hand decorating made Taos a huge success, c. 1985. (Complete listing in dinnerware price tables.)

Proprietary to Mervyn's stores, Mirage achieved a hand painted look in transferware, c. 1985. (See 1980s southwest style price tables.)

Country Styles

The plunge into dinnerware revealed a market void to Treasure Craft, and they sought to balance these modern lines with dinner and kitchenware designed to suit more provincial tastes. In 1984, Treasure Craft became a charter member and the sole ceramicist in the Center for Houseware Designs. CHD sought to cross-pollinate popular motifs into single patterns of fully coordinated housewares, complete with linens, glassware, paper products, wall art, and pottery.

Barth and Dreyfuss design director Bob Green contributed a line of kitchen towels adorned with country blue geese in ribbon bows. Treasure Craft and the other CHD members derived their *Ribbon Geese* pattern from this, introducing it as part of a complete coordinated table service in 1986. Ribbon Geese matched the newfound mania for country decorating in the mid-'80s, and joined Taos as a sales leader for Treasure Craft. Soon over a dozen country designs flourished in the company's catalogs, from cows and petit point hearts to floral designs in deep, rich reds, greens, and blues.

Hallmark (HMD) card and gift stores became an important new client, and they supplied a range of designs as possibilities for table and dinnerware. Treasure Craft licensed homey pieces created by HMD's designer Susan Marie McChesney and added them to the *Auntie Em* line. *Linden Ivy* and other attractive, studied floral patterns from Hallmark would follow.

With Franciscan gone and Metlox in decline, Treasure Craft filled the void, experimenting with many smaller sets of dinnerware. An enlarged in-house design team translated a floral watercolor by product development director Janet Scheer-Parks into kitchenware, while director Nina Dooley's abstract jewel tone sprays graced Treasure Craft kitchen accessories. Amy Way and Shou-I Sun were other designers who contributed to Treasure Craft's burgeoning lines.

Derived from designer Bob Green's pattern for Barth and Dreyfuss linens, Ribbon Geese was a cooperative effort to match other manufacturers' wall decor and accessories. (See 1980s country pattern tables.)

Cameo Rose was made for Hallmark based on one of their 1980s designs. (See standard blanks tables.)

Cookie Jars & Collectables

Novelty cookie jars, pitchers, and bowls were sculpted to match standard dinnerware lines in the late 1980s. Sold with Seascape, Paradise Collection, and Pacifica patterns were these designs by Chen: *Fish* cookie jars, 10.5", $28-32; Platter, 14", $22-27; Teapot, 7", $25-30; *Toucan* cookie jar, 10.5", $35-40; Pitcher, 8", $28-32; Leaf platter, 14", $18-24; Shells cookie jar, 10.5", $32-38.

Greenhouse by Treasure Craft designer Nina Dooley in mid-'80s jewel tones. (See provincial pattern tables.)

Big Successes in the Big 80's 123

Modern styles not based on southwest motifs evolved. The small *Carnival* line of concentric ring kitchenware was produced, competing with Metlox Colorstax in cranberry, navy, and hunter green. Eye-popping seashore styles sold through Robert Redford's *Sundance* catalog. Sculpted cookie jars, pitchers, and shakers were styled as go-alongs, including a vibrant *Toucan* pitcher for the Caribbean influenced *Paradise Collection* and Dooley's popular *Saguaro Cactus* jars.

Expansion and Devastation

Treasure Craft's sudden success as a dinnerware producer forced major expansion. The Compton plant grew to a quarter million square feet, with over 400 employees operating on double shifts. "Everyone had to learn how to do everything just to keep up with it," explained Levin of those frantic days.

By October 1987, Treasure Craft enjoyed its greatest prosperity ever. Orders and production were surging as the holiday season approached. Then, calamity struck.

Bruce Levin recounted it this way:

"It was 7:42 in the morning, and everyone had reported for the day shift. We'd just fired all the kilns when we heard the usual roar of a big truck passing the factory—except it didn't stop. The shaking started to get more violent, and some of the workers who'd lived through the Mexico City earthquake started running for the exits."

The workers were right; the October 1, 1987 Whittier earthquake had begun. By its end, all thirty-four of the plant's huge envelope kilns were reduced to rubble. Amazingly, no one was seriously hurt, and somehow the still warming kilns didn't spread their fire through the plant.

Still, the effect could scarcely have been more disastrous, the most serious catastrophe to strike Treasure Craft since the fire of 1955. California's litigious climate had made earthquake insurance an impossibility for the high-risk pottery industry, so with just two months before Christmas, there was no chance to fill their holiday orders.

Treasure Craft seemed doomed. But just as in 1955, worker loyalty resurrected the plant. Workers helped clean up the huge mess, salvaging what they could, and new tunnel kilns with heavier spacer blocks were installed to resist future quakes.

Meanwhile, Levin set about notifying his accounts of the bad news. With nothing left to lose, he audaciously set out to convince clients not just to maintain their holiday orders, but to prepay a portion so Treasure Craft could rebuild.

The gambit worked. "Amazingly, our vendors had enough faith in us to pay in advance for stock they wouldn't get until after the season was over!" Levin exclaimed. Relationships that had lasted decades transcended mere bottom-line business, and other vendors followed suit. Incredibly, Treasure Craft was back to full production by early 1988.

Two views of the destruction inside Treasure Craft's factory after the October 1987 Whittier earthquake.

Teepee teapot, 8", $29-36.

Shi Yi Chen and the Sculpted Cookie Jars

The year 1987 saw another exciting development, as a new sculptor named Shi Yi Chen joined Treasure Craft as a contractor. After a long struggle, husband Jun, her daughter, and she persuaded the Chinese government to allow their exodus to America. Arriving in Los Angeles with the clothes on their back and the $120 emigrants were allowed to take from China, they moved in with a sponsoring relative and began calling ceramic factories looking for work.

Chen designed and sculpted a *Merry-Go-Round* cookie jar, then called on ten different potteries with no luck before she came to Compton. Treasure Craft was enjoying much success contracting with many different designers, and was eager to find an experienced sculptor with fresh ideas. "Ceramic companies needed two or three different sculptors for variety's sake," Chen remarked. Treasure Craft offered her a contract on the spot.

Sculptor Shi Yi Chen and her family left China with $120 to start a new life in America. Treasure Craft hired her on her arrival in 1987.

Design director Dooley applied Chen's talents to the burgeoning sculpted cookie jar line, with the *Cat with Fishbowl* among her first models. It immediately became the firm's best selling cookie jar. *Dinosaur* motifs were a craze among late '80s youngsters, and Chen sculpted a whimsical purple, blue, and grey set that included a teapot, pitcher, and shakers with the cookie holder.

A multi-colored fish and a sand castle jar matching the *Seascape* dinnerware line were other late '80s Chen contributions. She would go on to sculpt models for Treasure Craft's award winning Disney jars and limited edition lines in the 1990s.

Holding an Anchor-Hocking glass fish bowl, this cat cookie jar was Treasure Craft's leading 1980s novelty seller, 10.5", $24-28.

Chen's Dinosaur line appealed to dino-crazy kids in the late '80s. Pitcher, 10", $24-28; Cookiesaurus, 12", $32-38; Shakers, 4", $12-16; Teapot, 7", $28-32.

Big Successes in the Big 80's   125

Seeking Production Partners

Thriving and vital, Treasure Craft was nearing its zenith in 1988. Orders were so strong that Levin sought new partners to help meet demand for their dinnerware, which couldn't be produced fast enough. *Crafted with Pride in America* was important enough to Levin that the slogan appeared as a back stamp on most Treasure Craft pieces; accordingly, he sought an American dinnerware maker for additional production.

Local rival Metlox of Manhattan Beach was ailing, and its plant declared an EPA Superfund cleanup site; its 1989 demise was to leave Treasure Craft as California's last major pottery factory. So Levin instead contacted Pfaltzgraff, a 150 year old, family controlled concern based in York, Pennsylvania.

Pfaltzgraff was impressed by what they saw happening in Compton…so much so, they countered Levin's contract offer with a surprise offer to buy out Treasure Craft. On November 30, 1988, the family era of ownership ended, and Treasure Craft became a subsidiary of the Susquehanna Pfaltzgraff Company.

1980s Neo-Deco Styles

Pueblo candlesticks, one of several southwest geometric patterns, $18-20/pr.

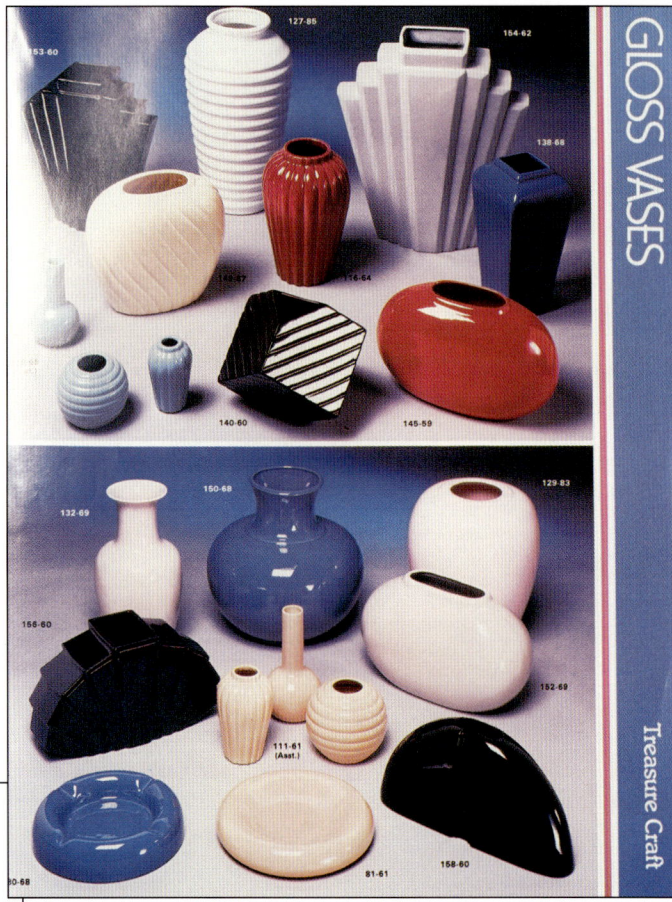

Fashion Vases in gloss and pastels, high style '80s deco. Though they were only made in Compton, a few wore Hawaiian foil labels after production on Maui ceased in 1984. Floor vases, $18-24/ea.; Squared geometrics, $24-30/ea.; Medium sizes, $12-18/ea.; Small sizes, $5-10/ea.; Ashtrays, $4-6/ea.

Masa Mami designer vase, c. 1984, 4.5", $20-24.

126   Big Successes in the Big 80's

1980s Dinnerware Patterns
Poppy and Butterfly, 1970s-1980s

Butterfly and Poppy became complete dinnerware lines in the 1980s.
Baking dish, $25-30.
Bowl, lug, $12-15.
Bowl, mixing, sm., $8-10.
Bowl, mixing, med., $10-12.
Bowl, mixing, lg., $12-15.
Butter dish/lid, $12-14.
Canister, bale, $10-12.
Canister, 7.5", $10-13.
Canster, 9.5", $12-15.
Canisters, sq., set of 5, $45-55/set.
Casserole, $15-18.
Cheese dome, $14-18.
Coasters, set of 8, $10-12/set.
Cookie jar, canister, $14-18.
Creamer, $5-7.
Egg plate, $15-19.
Honey pot/spinner, $14-16.
Lazy susan, 5-part, $20-24.
Mug, coffee, $7-9.
Pie or quiche pan, $12-16.
Pitcher, qt., $15-18.
Plaque, dealer, $12-15.
Plate, luncheon, $12-15.
Plate, dinner, $14-16.
Shakers, $7-9.
Scoop, $10-12.
Soap dish, $5-8.
Spoon rest, $7-10.
Sugar/lid, $7-9.
Teapot, 4-cup, $22-26.
Tile, $10-12.
Trivet, $8-10.
Tureen, lid/ladle, $40-50.
Utensil crock, $14-16.
Washstand set, $30-35.

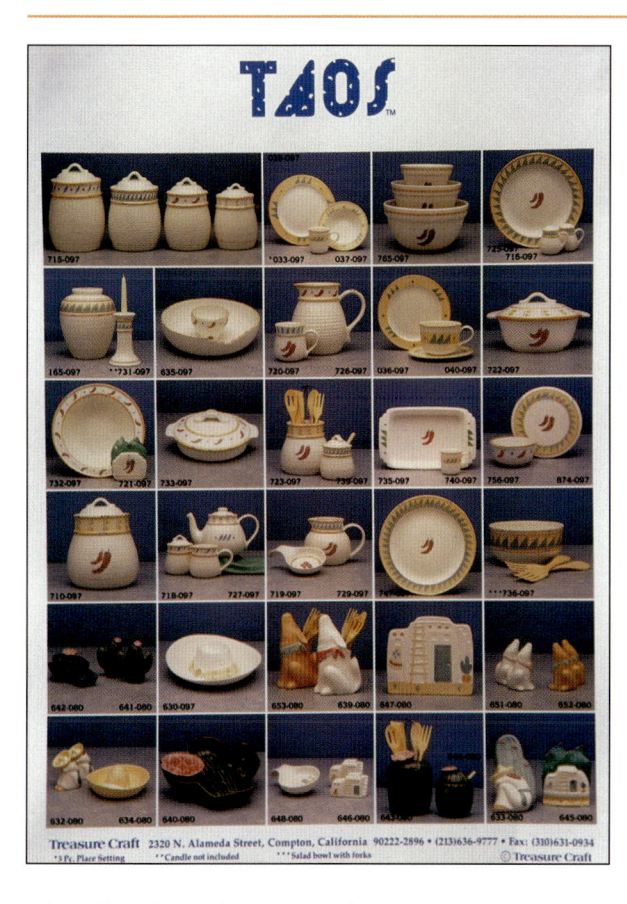

Southwestern Styles

Southwest luminara, c. 1987, $18-24. (Most of the line wore a lavender and grey transfer decal of a Navajo rug geometric pattern.)

Taos line, c. 1985.

Big Successes in the Big 80's

Saratoga, c. 1985.

Dinnerware on Standard Blanks

Paradise Collection's vivid mix-and-match patterns included Martinique, Kingston, Cozumel, and Montego, c. 1985.

Prices for Southwestern Dinnerware Patterns

	Taos	Southwest	Mirage	Saratoga
Baking dish	$55-65	$38-45	$30-35	
Bowl, batter	$42-48			
Bowl, cereal/chili	$7-9	$7-9	$6-8	$6-8
Bowl, lug		$8-10		
Bowl, rim soup	$12-15			$10-12
Bowl, mixing, qt.	$14-18	$14-18	$10-12	$10-12
Bowl, mixing, 1.5 qt.	$18-22	$18-22	$14-18	$13-15
Bowl, mixing, 2 qt.	$24-28	$20-24	$18-22	$17-19
Bowl, serving, sm.	$22-25			
Bowl, serving, lg.	$27-30			
Bowl, salad/utensils	$32-38	$22-25	$22-25	$20-24
Butter dish	$18-22	$18-22	$18-22	$16-20
Candlesticks, pr.	$35-40	$18-22	$18-22	
Carafe, four mugs			$25-32	
Canisters, bale, set of 3			$20-24	
Canister, sm.	$13-16	$12-14	$12-14	$10-12
Canister, med.	$15-18	$12-15		$12-14
Canister, lg.	$18-20	$12-15	$12-15	$12-15
Canister, xl.	$20-22	$13-16		$13-16
Casserole, sm.	$25-30	$20-24	$18-22	
Casserole, lg.	$39-45			
Chip & dip, hat		$15-18	$15-18	$13-15
Chip & dip, 2-part	$30-35	$30-35	$24-28	$15-24
Chip & dip, cactus	$20-25			
Condiment/spoon	$20-25			
Cookie canister	$24-26	$18-22	$18-22	$13-15
Cookie jar, novelty	$24-30	$20-25	$20-25	$28-45
Creamer	$10-12	$8-10	$6-8	$6-8
Luminaire		$18-20		
Mug, coffee	$6-8	$6-8	$5-7	
Mug, soup/liner	$8-12	$7-10	$6-8	$6-8
Napkin holder	$20-24	$15-20	$12-15	
Pitcher, pint	$12-15			
Pitcher, bulbous	$18-22	$16-20	$14-16	
Pitcher, qt.	$20-24	$18-20		
Pitcher, 2 qt.	$24-30	$24-28	$18-24	$18-22
Plate, salad	$6-8	$6-8	$6-8	$6-8
Plate, luncheon	$10-12	$8-10	$8-10	$8-10
Plate, dinner	$13-16	$12-14	$9-12	$10-12
Plate, chop, sm.	$18-22	$14-18	$14-18	$15-20
Plate, chop, lg.	$24-28			
Plaque, dealer	$15-20	$14-16	$14-18	
Potpourri/stand	$22-25	$18-24		
Relish, 3-section	$35-40			
Shakers, cyl./handled	$8-10	$7-9	$6-8	$5-7
Shakers, novelty	$12-20	$10-15	$9-13	
Spoon rest, reg.	$12-15	$8-10	$8-10	$10-13
Spoon rest, novelty	$15-20			
Sugar/lid	$10-12	$8-10	$7-9	$7-9
Teapot, 4-cup	$25-30	$24-26	$20-22	
Teapot, novelty				$27-35
Tortilla warmer	$30-36			
Trivet	$14-18	$13-16	$13-16	$12-15
Tumblers (glass)	$6-10	$4-8		
Utensil caddy, reg.	$14-18	$12-15	$10-14	$12-15
Utensil caddy, cactus	$18-24			
Vase, 8"	$18-24	$18-24		
Vase, 10"	$24-28			

Big Successes in the Big 80's

Bandana

Bandana pattern came in two color combinations, c. 1990.

Tivoli

Tivoli offered a traditional, hand decorated look on the ring blanks.

Prices for Other Concentric Ring Dinnerware

	Paradise Collection	Bandana	Tivoli
Baking dish			$28-35
Bowl, batter			$30-36
Bowl, cereal/chili			$6-8
Bowl, rim soup	$7-9	$8-10	$10-12
Bowl, mixing, qt.	$9-12	$10-12	$13-15
Bowl, mixing, 1.5 qt.	$10-14	$12-14	$14-16
Bowl, mixing, 2 qt.	$12-15	$14-16	$16-18
Bowl, serving, sm.	$10-14	$10-14	$14-17
Bowl, serving, lg.			$16-20
Bowl, salad/utensils	$18-22		$22-25
Butter dish/lid			$15-19
Candlesticks, pr.	$15-20		$18-22
Carafe, four mugs	$24-28		$24-28
Canisters, bale, set of 3			$24-30
Canister, sm.	$9-11	$10-12	$11-14
Canister, med.			$13-16
Canister, lg.	$12-14	$12-14	$14-18
Canister, xl.			$15-20
Casserole			$24-26
Chip & dip, 2-part	$18-24	$18-24	$20-25
Condiment/spoon			$14-16
Cookie canister	$12-15	$13-15	$16-20
Creamer		$6-8	$6-8
Mug, coffee		$5-7	$5-7
Mug, soup/liner			$7-10
Napkin holder			$12-15
Pitcher, pint	$7-9	$8-10	
Pitcher, bulbous	$10-14		$14-16
Pitcher, qt.	$13-15		
Pitcher, 2 qt.	$18-20	$20-22	$22-25
Plate, salad	$7-9	$7-9	
Plate, luncheon	$8-10	$8-10	$9-12
Plate, dinner	$11-13	$11-13	$12-14
Plate, chop, sm.	$13-16		$14-16
Plate, chop, lg.	$14-18		$18-20
Plaque, dealer			$12-15
Relish		$25-30	
Shakers	$6-8	$6-8	$6-8
Spoon rest	$7-9	$8-10	$8-10
Sugar/lid		$7-9	$7-9
Teapot, 4-cup	$20-22		
Trivet	$8-12		$10-14
Utensil caddy	$10-12	$12-14	$12-15
Vase, 8"			$14-16
Vase, 10"			$16-20
Vase, 15"			$24-28

Big Successes in the Big 80's

Country Transfer Dinnerware

1980s Table and Kitchen Accessories

Floral Patterns

Stitch in Time added place settings (on Pfaltzgraff blank shapes) to the Auntie Em Collection.

- Baking dish, $14-18.
- Bowl, cereal or chili, $5-7.
- Bowl, rim soup, $6-8.
- Bowl, mixing, qt., $8-10.
- Bowl, mixing, 1.5 qt., $10-12.
- Bowl, mixing, 2 qt., $12-14.
- Butter/lid, $12-15.
- Canister, sm., $7-9.
- Canister, lg., $8-10.
- Condiment/spoon, $9-12.
- Cookie canister, $10-12.
- Cookie jar, cat, $22-28.
- Creamer, $4-6.
- Cup, coffee, $3-5.
- Egg plate, $12-14.
- Mug, coffee, $3-5.
- Napkin holder, $8-12.
- Pie or quiche pan, $12-15.
- Pitcher, 2 qt., $14-16.
- Plaque, dealer, $7-9.
- Plate, salad, $5-7.
- Plate, luncheon, $7-9.
- Plate, dinner, $8-10.
- Plate, chop, $12-15.
- Shakers, $4-6.
- Spoon rest, $6-8.
- Sugar/lid, $4-6.
- Teapot, 4-cup, $14-18.
- Trivet, reg., $6-8.
- Trivet, novelty, $7-14.
- Tureen/ladle, $22-28.
- Utensil caddy, $8-10.

Linden Ivy, based on a Hallmark pattern, late 1980s.

French Village, late 1980s.

130 Big Successes in the Big 80's

Rosemarie

Rosemarie, c. 1985.

Dauphine

Dauphine, c. 1985.

Shenandoah

Shenandoah, c. 1990.

Prices for Other Patterns on Standard Blanks

	Cameo Rose	Americana Quilt	Chesapeake/ Avignon	Blue Mountain
Baking dish	$22-28			
Bowl, cereal or chili	$5-7	$5-7		
Bowl, rim soup		$6-8	$8-10	$10-12
Bowl, mixing, qt.	$9-12	$8-10	$10-12	
Bowl, mixing, 1.5 qt.	$10-14	$9-12	$10-14	
Bowl, mixing, 2 qt.	$12-15	$10-13	$12-16	
Bowl, serving	$14-16			
Bowl, salad/utensils	$18-22	$14-18	$20-24	$20-24
Canisters, bale, set of 3	$20-30			
Canister, sm.	$9-12	$7-10	$9-12	$12-14
Canister, lg.	$10-14	$8-12	$12-15	$13-16
Casserole	$20-24			
Chip & dip, 2-part	$14-16	$12-15	$18-20	$18-20
Condiment/spoon	$10-13			
Cookie canister	$12-15	$10-13	$13-16	$14-18
Cookie jar, novelty		$22-30		
Creamer	$5-7	$4-6	$6-8	
Egg plate	$12-14			
Lazy Susan, 5-part	$20-24			
Mug, coffee	$4-6	$3-5	$5-7	$5-7
Napkin holder	$8-12		$12-15	
Pie or quiche pan	$14-16			
Pitcher, 2 qt.	$18-20	$14-16	$20-24	$20-24
Plate, salad	$7-9			
Plate, luncheon	$9-11	$7-9	$10-12	$10-12
Plate, dinner	$10-12	$8-10	$12-15	$12-15
Plate, chop, sm.	$12-15	$10-13	$14-18	$14-18
Plate, chop, lg.			$15-20	$15-20
Plate, serving, sq.				$30-35
Platter	$15-18			
Plaque, dealer	$10-14			
Relish, tri-part	$15-20			
Shakers, reg.	$5-7	$4-6	$6-8	$6-8
Shakers, novelty		$8-12		
Spoon rest	$7-9	$5-7	$8-10	$9-12
Sugar/lid	$7-9	$5-7	$8-10	
Teapot, 4-cup	$18-20	$15-18	$22-25	
Trivet	$9-14		$10-14	
Tureen/ladle	$24-30			
Utensil caddy	$9-12	$6-9	$10-13	$12-14

Big Successes in the Big 80's

Early 80s Provincial Kitchenware

Blossoms, c. 1985.

Country Inns, c. 1985.

Alouette, 1985.

Cook's Nook c. 1985.

1980s Country Kitchenware

Ribbon Geese was a smash with country decorators when it came out in 1986.

Auntie Em lines included several variations on the country theme, sold under different pattern names.

Big Successes in the Big 80's   133

Prices for 1980s Country and Provincial Kitchenware

Baking dish, $14-20.
Bowl, batter, $20-25.
Bowl, lug, $5-7.
Bowl, mixing, qt., $8-10.
Bowl, mixing, 1.5 qt., $10-12.
Bowl, mixing, 2 qt., $12-14.
Bowl, salad/utensils, $16-20.
Box, heart, $8-12.
Canisters, bale, set of 3, $18-24.
Canister, sm., $6-8.
Canister, lg., $8-10.
Casserole, sm., $13-18.
Casserole, lg., $14-20.
Casserole, novelty, $29-35.
Cheese dome, $14-18.
Chamberstick, $12-18.
Chip & dip, hat, $14-18.
Coasters, set of 8, $8-10.
Cookie canister, $10-12.
Cookie jar, novelty, $18-25.
Dish, heart $7-10.
Egg plate, $12-15.
Lazy susan, 5 piece, $18-22.
Mug, coffee, $3-5.
Napkin holder, $10-15.
Pie or quiche pan, reg., $9-11.
Pie or quiche, heart, $12-15.
Pitcher, pint, $6-8.
Pitcher, qt., $8-12.
Plaque, dealer, $8-10.
Plaque, wall, $8-12.
Plate, chop, $10-14.
Salt box, wood, $12-15.
Shakers, reg., $4-6.
Shakers, novelty, $8-12.
Spoon rest, $5-7.
Teapot, 2-cup, $12-15.
Teapot, 4-cup, $15-18.
Tile, $9-12.
Trivet, $7-9.
Tureen/ladle, $22-28.
Utensil caddy, $8-10.
Washstand set, sm., $14-18.
Washstand set, lg., $24-28.

1980s Modern Kitchenware

Horizon and Images, kitchenware variations of the popular Mirage decorating style.

1980s Cookie Jars

Sculpted cookie jars, early 1980s. *Top row:* Girl in bonnet, $22-28; Football boy, $30-40; Grandma, $27-32. *Second row:* Slot machine, $50-55; Ice Cream Cone, $40-50; Gumball machine, $35-40. *Bottom row:* Fish bowl bear, $25-30; Fish bowl pig, $28-32; Cat with Fish Bowl, early version, $28-32; Teddy Bear Fish Bowl, $25-30.

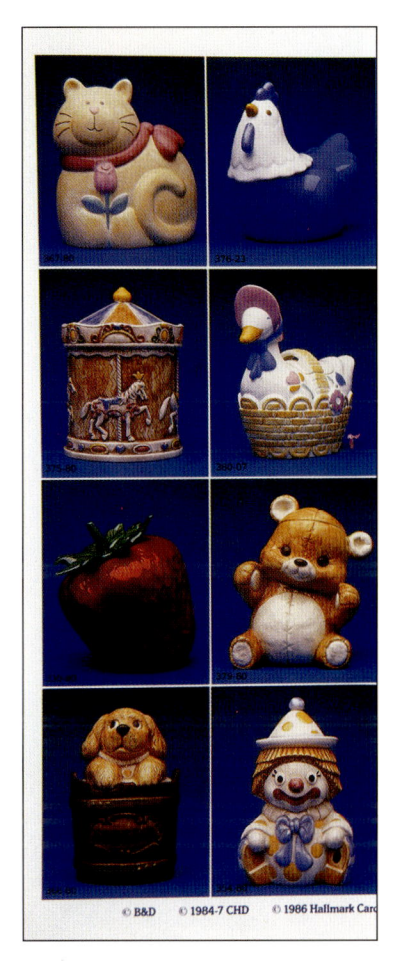

Three decades of cookie jar design are shown on this 1980s photo panel. Cat with Tulip by Susan Marie McChesney, $30-35; Blue Hen, $24-28; Merry-Go-Round by Chen, 1987, $30-35; Blue Belle goose, $24-28; Strawberry, $30-35; Stitch Bear by Winton, $25-28; Puppy in Barrel, update of 1960s design, $24-28; Clown, late 1970s design, $25-30.

Treasure Craft's move to more colorful jars delighted cookie jar collectors in the early '80s. Country Critters, $29-35/ea. Pet Shop, $32-38/ea.

Big Successes in the Big 80's

Famous Amos commissioned cookie jar bags and banks from Treasure Craft in the early '80s. Jars, antique or natural, $28-35. Banks, $22-28.

Snowman and Santa fish bowl belly style jars, late 1980s, $30-40.

All-Star Jars, a popular 1980s line, all 8.5": Golf ball, $45-50; Tennis ball, $55-65; Soccer ball, $50-60; Football, $50-60; Bowling ball, $45-50; Baseball, $50-60; Basketball, $50-60; Eight ball, $75-85.

136   Big Successes in the Big 80's

Restyled Jukebox, c. 1990 (slightly smaller than late '70s version), $45-50.

Don Winton's Noah's Ark jar was so popular that it lasted a quarter-century in the line, 1970s-1990s, $24-30.

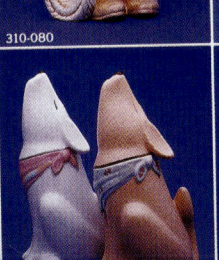

A full line of western novelty cookie jars grew to augment Treasure Craft's popular southwestern dinnerware styles. *Top row:* Teepee, $30-35; Covered Wagon, $40-45; Cowboy, $40-45; Medicine Bear, $27-32. *Bottom row:* Boots, $30-35/ea.; Bandana Cactus, $30-35; Coyotes (white matched Mirage, tan for Southwest), $24-30; Siesta, $28-35.

Tombstone Radio jar, late 1980s, $45-50.

Big Successes in the Big 80's   137

The Pfaltzgraff Era: 1988-1995

Pfaltzgraff's purchase of Treasure Craft in late 1988 seemed the perfect marriage. Both had built from small family-owned businesses into major pottery firms, prospering through decades of decline in a difficult business. Both had successful dinnerware lines, and Pfaltzgraff's traditional styles were nicely rounded out by Treasure Craft's contemporary and country patterns. The York, Pennsylvania, firm's major accounts in the east and Treasure Craft's in the west offered untold opportunity for both lines to expand.

Treasure Craft blanks covered a wide range of decorative accessories Pfaltzgraff could not make, which could be easily decorated to match the dinnerware made in York. In turn, the York plants were structured for high production of place settings, which Treasure Craft needed to fill orders that were stretching it to the limit. In 1989, *A Pfaltzgraff Company* appeared on Treasure Craft sales sheets, and some back stamps as well.

Treasure Craft's Pinocchio and Cleo cookie jar won Disney's worldwide award for best three-dimensional licensed character in 1991, 13", $55-65.

Integrating the two potteries required new technical mastery at Treasure Craft, whose canister and tableware styles were rakish and streamlined compared to the scalloped ware made in York. New master molds were sculpted to match Pfaltzgraff designs, with twisted rope handles and undulating forms, requiring extra steps in casting and application. To the parent firm's surprise, Treasure Craft executed them skillfully, quickly matching Pfaltzgraff dinnerware patterns.

Dinnerware and Pattern Matching

Garden Party was Treasure Craft's first accessory line designed to match Pfaltzgraff place settings. The hand-painted, embossed lines and rope handles were laborious to design and make. (See table at end of chapter for pieces and pricing.)

Garden Party and *Silhouette* were two such patterns now accessorized by Treasure Craft. These popular, deeply embossed floral patterns were laborious to make, but opened up Dillards, Williams-Sonoma, and other high-end housewares stores to Treasure Craft's lines. Treasure Craft extended their use with *Somerset*, created for Hallmark based on its proprietary floral pattern.

Treasure Craft also perfected the gloss-on-matte black glazes Pfaltzgraff used on its fashionable *Midnight Sun* pattern, defying the parent firm's predictions that it couldn't be replicated in California. A stunning contrast of shiny, abstract geometric designs shone from a satin background, sealed with the clear matte overglaze developed for the Taos line in the 1980s. Midnight Sun was a natural for Treasure Craft's handsome stair-stepped chip and dip set, candle pillars, and serving platters.

In retrospect, these technical achievements created huge problems for Treasure Craft. As the economy suddenly slumped during the 1989 holidays, Pfaltzgraff became alarmed that their new subsidiary might take sales from the parent firm by producing accessories for its lines. Treasure Craft could no longer create go-alongs for Pfaltzgraff lines at will, restricted to producing items requested by the management in York. In the end, only a handful of Pfaltzgraff lines would ever be combined with accessories from Compton.

Nor did Pfaltzgraff show excitement for producing dinnerware pieces to fill out Treasure Craft's newer dinnerware lines. NOT AVAILABLE was superimposed on an increasing number of plates and bowls on Treasure Craft catalog pages, severely limiting the chance to reach new accounts. This became especially critical in 1993, when Mervyn's canceled expansion plans (and orders for its proprietary Mirage dinnerware) in the face of California's worst recession in a generation.

"Not Available" began to spring up on place settings in Treasure Craft catalogues as Pfaltzgraff focused on their York, Pennsylvania, designs during the Gulf War recession.

A Return to Hand Decoration

Faced with these problems and the 1990 Gulf War oil price shocks, Treasure Craft did what had always worked in the past—they created new lines. At Pfaltzgraff's behest, Bruce Levin had agreed to stay with the California operation for five years, so he called on the parent firm to help extend the Midnight Sun black into a new line of accessories. Pfaltzgraff designer David Walsh devised a set of ten vases, serving trays, and bowls called *Origins*, with impressed black geometric designs in off-white borders. The impact was stark and handsome, evocative of the intaglio work of Navajo Indian pots. Added were molds from Treasure Craft's seminal 1970s Pueblo line, using tan glaze with black highlighting to simulate woven coil baskets.

Midnight Sun accessories also matched an existing Pfaltzgraff line. Their difficult gloss-on-satin monochrome was a true accomplishment for Treasure Craft's decorators, and have continued to be sought in the after market. (Pitcher, 2 qt., $55-65.)

Pfaltzgraff designer David Walsh created the stunning Origins line for Treasure Craft, utilizing the Midnight Sun glazes, c. 1990. Vases, 8" and 14", $22-25 and $40-50; Chop plate, 16", $30-35; Square serving dish, 15", $45-50; Serving bowl, 12", $24-28; Serving bowl, 16", $30-35; Baskets, derived from 1970s Pueblo molds: 6", $12-15, 8", $22-25, 12", $28-32, 16", $40-45.

The Pfaltzgraff Era: 1988-1995

Since place settings were still difficult to produce, Treasure Craft devised hand-painted patterns that would sell in smaller numbers at higher prices. *Avignon* and *Chesapeake* featured bold brush strokes, while the brushed florals of *Tivoli* were a soft alternative to the firm's precise floral decal lines. *Bandana* and *Blue Mountain* extended the southwest styles, cast from hand thrown prototypes to emulate wheel thrown pots. Their bulbous canister and pitcher shapes required slow, costly slip casting, and production was low. Chic and expensive, they reached few cost conscious consumers during the early '90s recession.

Lacking additional plate blanks from York, Treasure Craft chose to replace high volume transfer ware with more exclusive hand-painted dinnerware lines.

Disney and the Sculpted Cookie Jars

One area where Treasure Craft had free rein was the sculpted lines of cookie jars, teapots, and shaker sets shaped by design director Nina Dooley, Shi Yi Chen, and other Treasure Craft sculptors. Whether vintage or new, novelty cookie jars were wildly popular collectables in the early '90s, and Treasure Craft extended their line with several fun new shapes. A *Dog on Sled* led a group of holiday jars, while Chen's '50s-style pickup truck jars drove past Treasure Craft castles on American kitchen counters. Treasure Craft's *Cookie Time* alarm clock jar even rested in the kitchen of the hit TV show *Friends*.

A pair of rag dolls appeared as a teapot and cookie jar. *Sugar* was a white doll, *Spice* had black skin tone. Industry watchers warned Bruce Levin that a black girl cookie jar would cause controversy, but he saw it differently. "I figured black kids probably wanted to play with black dolls, so Nina and I just made sure they were represented identically." J.C. Penney agreed, and so did the public, eagerly snapping them up in the early '90s.

Dog on Sled cookie jar, one of several fun designs that appeared briefly in the early '90s, 11.5", $45-50.

Treasure Craft's Cookie Time clock found a home in the kitchen of the hit show *Friends*, c. 1992, 11", $28-32.

140   The Pfaltzgraff Era: 1988-1995

Sugar and Spice were black and white rag doll look-alikes designed by Bruce Levin and Nina Dooley, early '90s. Sugar (white): Cookie jar, 14.5", $35-45; Teapot, 9", $32-38. Spice (black): Cookie jar, $85-100; Teapot, $65-75; Shakers (both girls), 3.75", $24-28.

Also in 1990, a strong twenty-year relationship culminated in Disney's licensing of standard characters to Treasure Craft. Likenesses of *Dopey*®, *Goofy*®, and other Disney favorites could now be sculpted into cookie jars and tableware, and sold to accounts outside the theme parks for the first time.

Disney licensed Treasure Craft to turn current movie characters into three-dimensional tableware in the early '90s. Not shown elsewhere: *Mrs. Potts*®: cookie jar, 10", $45-55, Teapot, 7.5", $29-36, Bank, 6", $22-28. *Seven Dwarfs*®: Utensil caddy, 8", $25-32, *Dopey*® cookie jar, 14.5", $80-90, *Doc*® teapot, 10", $30-40, Shakers, 3.75", $20-24. *101 Dalmations*®: Cookie, 13", $32-39, Canister, 9", $20-25, Pitcher, 11", $24-30, Shakers, 3.5", $20-24, Teapot, 7.5", $29-35. *Aladdin*®: *Genie*® (profile) cookie jar, 13.5", $50-60, Teapot, 8", $39-45, Bank, 5.5", $24-30.

First of these new jars was Chen's design for *Pinocchio and Cleo*® the fish. Treasure Craft's hand-poured, hand-painted figure held an Anchor-Hocking glass bowl, topped with a simple ram-pressed lid with a brightly painted fish finial. Ingenious and inexpensive, the appealing new design so impressed Disney that Treasure Craft won the animator's award for *Best Three-Dimensional Licensed Product* in 1991, beating all other products in all categories worldwide.

Disney's approval brought a new contract to design novelty ware related to their current animated feature films, and Chen brought them to life. The *Mrs. Potts*® teapot from *Beauty and the Beast*® was the first to leap from the screen to the kitchen table, followed by two varieties of *Aladdin*® genie cookie jars, shakers, and a teapot. The full-figured genie jar earned Treasure Craft a spot on the front page of the *Los Angeles Times* entertainment section in 1992.

Chen later designed a dead-ringer likeness of the *Bulldog Café*, the real 1930s Los Angeles roadside restaurant seen in Disney's *The Rocketeer*®. From *The Nightmare Before Christmas*® came *Jack's Tomb*®, which sold well despite an inaugural price of $200 in 1993.

All this attention to cookie jars brought Treasure Craft another licensing agreement, this time to cast *Muppet*® figures in ceramic. A number of firms commissioned limited editions (chronicled later in this book); other editions proved limited due to their complexity. *Katrina*, designed to celebrate the fall of the Berlin Wall, was styled as a Russian stacking doll; her black glaze was hard to fire without burning her red cape, and few were made.

Rocketeer® jar sculpted by Shi Yi Chen, a faithful depiction of *The Dog Café* on Washington Boulevard in Los Angeles, 10", c. 1993, $70-80.

The Pfaltzgraff Era: 1988-1995

Jack Skellington's® Tombstone jar from *The Nightmare Before Christmas*®, oblique angle showing his ghost dog Zero® on the side, 16", c. 1993. Values have remained near its initial sales price of $200.

Gourmet Mickey transfer ware could fill an entire kitchen in the early '90s. Shakers (one shown), 5", $15-18. Teapot, 4-cup, $25-29. Bowl, mixing, 3", $15-18. Trivet, 6", $15-18. Canister with bale, 7", $15-18. Bell (not shown), $15-18.

Writing on the Wall

But even as Treasure Craft found success in new niches, Pfaltzgraff fretted over its subsidiary, whose size and structure demanded greater production. Increasing layers of management arrived from Pennsylvania, in hopes that more financial control and cost cutting would make the integration a success.

The new direction was made clear with an attempt to obtain low-cost trainees from Mexico, claiming that there were not enough trained ceramicists in the L.A. basin. A landmark pro-labor ruling in 1992 denied the claim, and Pfaltzgraff began to seek other ways to cut labor costs. Disheartened, the Levin family cut all ties in 1993.

Into the vacuum came new manager Paul Helgesen from York. Sculpting was applied to the remaining dinnerware blanks, resulting in solid color patterns like *Sanibel*, its arched edges glazed in jewel tones, and a cream ware line with grey glazed leaf handles. Sculpted tableware also accompanied the Disney film *Pocahontas*®, with carved petroglyphs set in relief.

With the passage of 1994's NAFTA free trade agreement, Pfaltzgraff set up a Mexican factory and began to send Treasure Craft molds there for production. This included several styles of cookie jars that had been American made, including the new *Bart Simpson*® jar, *Fozzie the Bear*®, and others. Problems surfaced immediately; an anonymous source witnessed a truckload of "whorishly painted" Mexican *Snow White*® jars being eagerly destroyed by Compton workers in the parking lot of that facility. Though some noteworthy limited editions continued to be made in California through 1995, staff morale and production were clearly failing.

So it was that in September 1995, Treasure Craft's California plant was closed. Most of the master molds were destroyed at Pfaltzgraff's behest, save for a few tableware blanks and some Disney and character lines, which were shipped to China. Outsourced to factories that continued to produce them as Treasure Craft, Pfaltzgraff hoped to satisfy the California firm's accounts. Their in-house publication claimed this would transform Treasure Craft into a moneymaker, though longtime executive secretary Joyce Brinks insisted that the California operation was profitable to the end.

Many of Treasure Craft's skilled designers were hired to work in-house at Disney, while others continued to freelance. Chen gave her reason for not following Treasure Craft to Pfaltzgraff's offshore plants; "The traditional ceramic culture has been lost. We didn't want to crank out low quality, flimsy ceramics".

The closure certainly reduced management headaches for York while removing a major player from the industry, yet it somehow failed to make Treasure Craft an asset to Pfaltzgraff. One plant manager confided that the total savings of offshore production amounted to just $1 per cookie jar.

By 1997, all remaining molds and the rights to the Treasure Craft name were sold to the management group Pfaltzgraff had installed, and the Mexican plant was closed shortly thereafter.

China's brand new factories made nice looking pottery at low cost, but five decades of goodwill and established buyer relationships were lost forever. Curt Blanchard styled several attractive new limited edition cookie jars for the *Gallery Collection*, but many new production lines were made before orders were secured. Glutted with overproduction, Treasure Craft's manager-owners only lasted eighteen months before being forced to sell to Zak Productions, a Spokane, Washington, import company, which discontinued all ceramic production in January 2003. Today, the Treasure Craft name is applied to school supplies made in China.

Bart Simpson® cookie jars were made in America for just one year, so USA-marked varieties have proven scarce, 1995, 14.5", $100-120.

Pocohontas® chop plate, one of the last Treasure Craft pieces made for Disney in California, 15", c. 1995, $32-38.

Oval platter with sculpted leaf handles, 1994-1995 only, 17", $22-28.

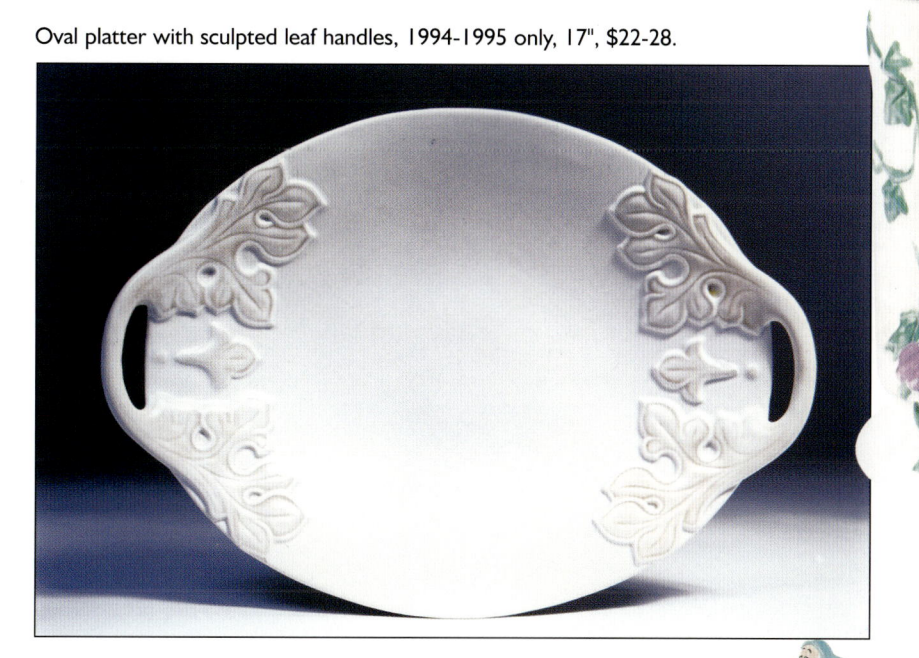

Miss Piggy® on Column cookie jar, another item made only briefly in America, c. 1994, 13", $55-65.

The Pfaltzgraff Era: 1988-1995

Epilogue

I was surprised to suddenly see Treasure Craft pieces marked DISCONTINUED all over Centralia, Washington's, Pfaltzgraff outlet one day in September 1995. A call to Joyce Brinks confirmed the sad realization that the firm's five decades of California production were over. "This never would have happened if the Levins had still been here," she wailed.

But Bruce Levin viewed it differently in hindsight. Still a potter, he moved his Justice Designs Group back into the old Treasure Craft plant after Pfaltzgraff left it in 1995. Levin chose to avoid overseas competition, producing wall sconces and custom lighting which feature time consuming incising, hand-rubbed finishes, and other costly specifications. Of his staff of thirty-two, thirteen came from Treasure Craft, some with three decades of service.

"We could never recreate what we had going at Treasure Craft now," Levin contended. "There was so much to do, so many things happening at once. Our culture has changed, and it would be hard to find people willing to do all the things it took to run a major pottery."

"China's regained leadership in ceramics because they're willing to make anything in any material Americans want. They're investing in plant, education, and people for the long-term, not like the grab and run Western approach. Once you've seen the quality and scale the new Chinese factories offer at such cheap prices, it's hard to imagine that everything won't be made there soon."

"Most of the American factories that have made it are in niches like Justice Designs. We've survived by doing things that are too hard to automate, and taking orders too small to be bothered with by the factors overseas. But the days of large American industrial plants have neared their end."

With that, there has proven to be little danger for collectors that American-made Treasure Craft will be recreated. In fact, only a handful of original master molds were spared destruction…four in California, a dozen in Hawaii, perhaps a few dozen in China. The rest of Treasure Craft's designs have survived only in collections of the pottery medley that grew from a little house in Gardena.

1990s Patterns
Treasure Craft Patterns on Pfaltzgraff Rope-Handled Shapes

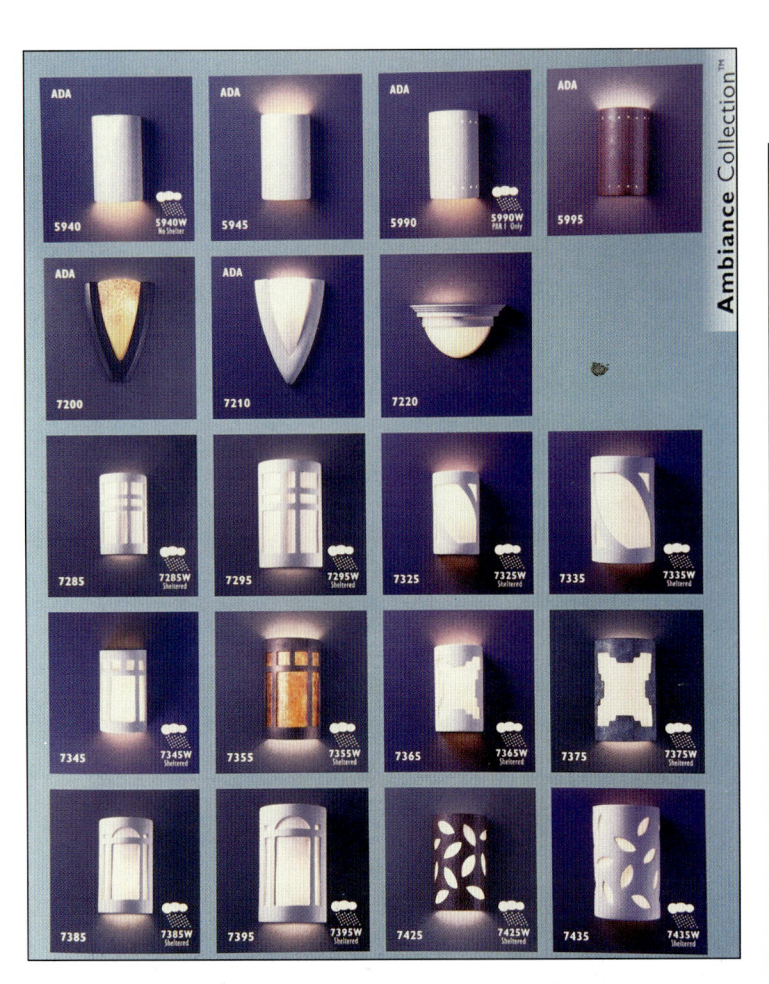

After Pfaltzgraff closed Treasure Craft's California plant, Bruce Levin's Justice Designs Group restarted it as a maker of ceramic-bodied specialty lighting. A third of the Justice staff used to work for Treasure Craft.

Somerset, c. 1990.

Silhouette, an unadorned variant on the embossed Garden Party pattern, c. 1990.

Pricing and Pieces Available on Rope Handle Blanks
(as of now, prices only established for Garden Party pattern)

	Garden Party	Pacifica	Silhouette	Somerset
Bowl, serving	$20-23	x	x	x
Cake pedestal	$24-28			
Candlesticks, pr.	$24-26			
Canister, sm.	$14-16	x	x	x
Canister, med.	$15-18	x	x	x
Canister, lg.	$18-20	x	x	x
Canister, xl.	$20-22	x	x	x
Chip & dip, 2-part	$20-24	x	x	x
Cookie canister	$20-24	x	x	x
Cookie jar, novelty	$24-28			
Creamer	$8-10	x		x
Mug, coffee		x	x	x
Napkin holder		x		x
Pitcher, 2 qt.		x	x	x
Plate, chop, sm.	$15-18	x	x	x
Plate, chop, lg.	$18-22	x		x
Planter	$14-16			
Shakers		x	x	x
Spoon rest	$10-14	x	x	x
Sugar/lid	$10-12	x		x
Teapot, 4-cup	$24-28	x		x
Utensil caddy	$15-18	x	x	x
Vase	$15-18			

Pacifica included patterns Monterey, Catalina, and Carmel, c. 1990.

1990s Dinnerware Patterns
(see previous chapter for piece and value listings)

Avignon was a chic, costly hand-painted dinnerware line, early 1990s.

Americana Quilt was designed outside Treasure Craft, c. 1990.

Blue Mountain accessories included blue versions of some Origins serving ware, c. 1990.

146   The Pfaltzgraff Era: 1988-1995

Late Production Pieces

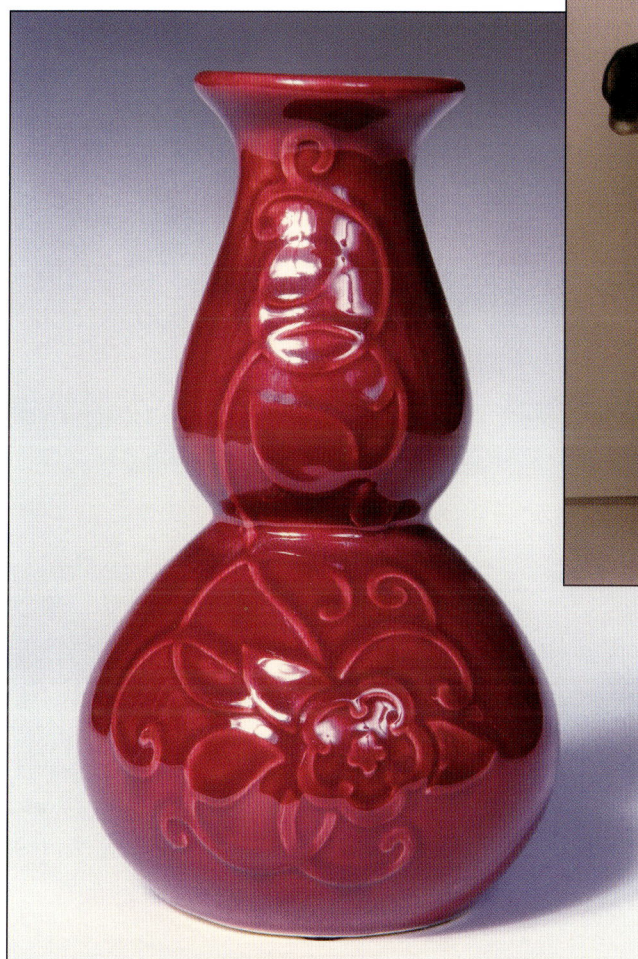

Cranberry embossed vase, late production, 8", $12-18.

Prototype Doc teapot wore slightly different colors than the final version, c. 1990, 9", $50-60.

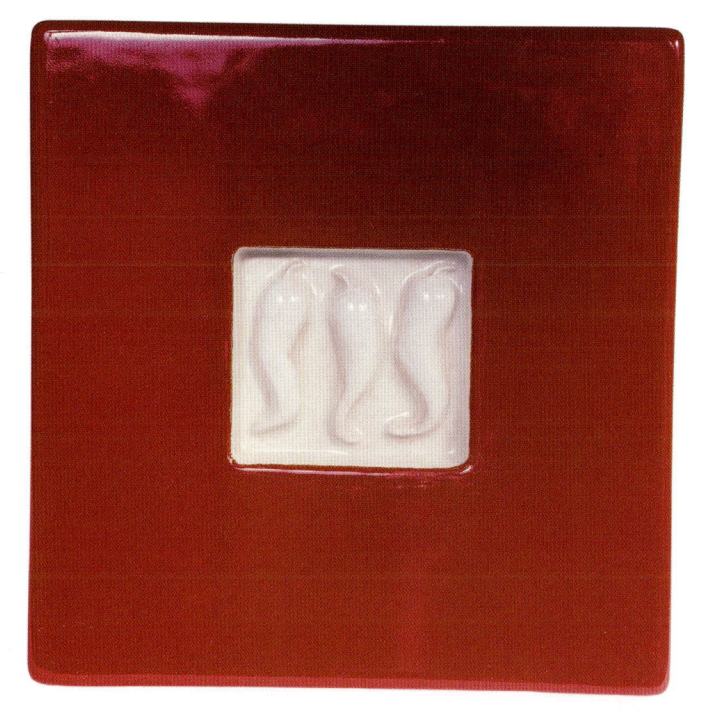

Embossed tile from late Treasure Craft production, c. 1995, 6", $8-12.

Sleepy® trivet came late enough to help put Treasure Craft USA to rest, c. 1995, 9.5", $24-28.

The Pfaltzgraff Era: 1988-1995   147

Limited Edition Cookie Jars: 1991-1995

A wave of nostalgia for early movie and television characters crested in the 1980s and '90s. Novelty cookie jars from the baby boom era were suddenly hot collectables, the more whimsical the better. Collectors desired new treatments of old characters that hadn't been memorialized in 1950s cookie jars.

Animation

Treasure Craft's award-winning Pinocchio® jar garnered a lot of attention for their sculpted, hand-decorated cookie jar lines. In 1991, a New York organization called Animation, headed by James Morrison and John DeSalvo, commissioned a limited edition of 500 jars and twenty-five promotional proofs depicting *Droopy the Dog*® of cartoon fame.

Facing tough times, Treasure Craft was glad to make a labor-intensive, high dollar item that required strict attention to detail by its decorators. Droopy's red color was slightly different than Pinocchio's, difficult to fire with the high-temperature black without burning; these obstacles were overcome, and the first run was underway.

But Animation failed to overcome its own obstacles, going out of business before the run was completed in 1992. Fewer than 200 were made; but Treasure Craft also made a new discovery. A truly limited edition could sell for hundreds. "We could take orders for as few as a hundred, let our decorators and finishers really spend time on them, and make money on something really well made," Bruce Levin constructed.

Treasure Craft experimented with other jars like *Katrina* (only 109 jars made) and *Jack's Tomb*, intricately designed and selling for prices up to $200. Director Tim Burton was pleased enough to order his production staff a special edition of 100, bearing his thanks and his signature on the back of the lid.

Around 100 of the *Nanna* black matron cookie jars were made in green dress (much scarcer than the thousands in production blue), and a few prototype gloss glazes proved to be one-of-a-kind. Just as he left Treasure Craft in 1993, Bruce Levin signed a limited edition of 125 *Old Red Truck* jars at the request of cookie jar maven Ellen Supnick.

Droopy®, Treasure Craft's first officially limited edition jar, 1991, $200-250.

Director Tim Burton commissioned a signature edition of 100 Jack Skellington's Tombstone jars, c. 1993, $300-400.

Katrina celebrated the fall of the Berlin Wall, c. 1991. Though not intended as a limited edition, the difficulty of firing red with black made her hard to make, and short-lived; under 100 were finished at the factory, $300-400.

Nanna in green dress, a color test of 300 pieces (production pieces were blue), early '90s, $150-175.

Limited Edition Cookie Jars: 1991-1995 149

McMe Productions

But Treasure Craft didn't seriously pursue numbered limited edition cookie jars until Pfaltzgraff took other lines away from Compton in 1994. Earlier that year, the Northridge earthquake had halted production at a small ceramic producer in the San Fernando Valley, who was under contract to produce a *Roy Rogers* cookie jar for McMe Productions. (Treasure Craft had learned from the disastrous 1987 earthquake, and was spared serious harm.)

McMe Productions was founded by avid collectors Gerald and Lonna McGee-Meyer of Simi Valley, whose love for novelty cookie jars and western heroes came together when they met with Roy Rogers in 1993. Never before the subject of a novelty jar, he gladly agreed to license his image to the fledgling designers.

With decades of cookie jar experience, Treasure Craft was an obvious choice. "Cookie jar collectors presumed that Treasure Craft meant good quality, so we figured their jars would sell as limited editions," Lonna added.

The designers montaged photo images and the profile cast in Rogers' 1950s F&F plastic mug into an accurate portrayal of the cowboy star, and Treasure Craft sculpted the bust. Upon approval for production, Roy signed it on the back when it was ready to be cast into a master mold. The copyright information would be decaled and the editions number painted on the bottom of each jar.

"Roy's was the first cookie jar based on an actual living person, rather than a fictional character," Lonna asserted. "That meant getting his facial features and highlights right would be tough." It took painstaking effort, but Arturo Garcia, head of the glaze department in Compton, perfected the colors. The pottery had the jars to market in just two months.

Made by Treasure Craft, McMe Productions' edition of 1100 Roy Rogers cookie jar busts sold out quickly at $159 apiece.

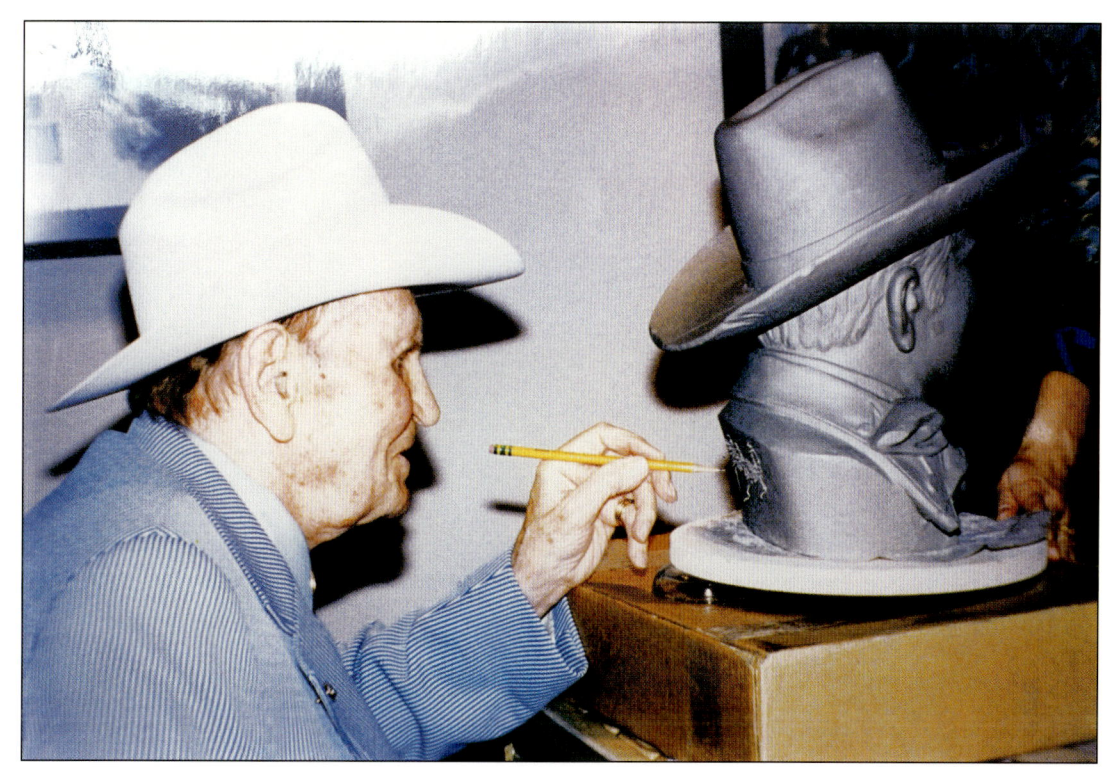

Roy Rogers signing the bust from which his cookie jar was made, 1994.

Good design, a popular subject, and Treasure Craft's name helped sell the edition of 1100 quickly at $159 each. *Dale Evans* was next to receive the treatment; after Evans signed the sculpture, a 400-piece edition was made.

Dale Evans cookie jar, 1994 edition of 400, $150-200.

Detail of signature on rear collar.

Limited Edition Cookie Jars: 1991-1995 151

"If a piece was broken or rejected in production, it would be tossed out and the number never reused," Gerald explained.

Cartoonist Cathy Guisewite was the licensing agent for Rogers and Evans. Pleased to approve the Rogers and Evans pieces, she encouraged McMe productions to produce a jar of her namesake character *Cathy*®. Treasure Craft's Shi Yi Chen, sculptor of many of the Disney lines, was chosen to craft a bust from drawings supplied by Guisewite's studio.

Cathy had been represented on a decidedly average, flat-faced jar made abroad in the 1980s, so Chen's faithful interpretation of the comic strip was a pleasant surprise to the usually reserved animator. "I always wondered what she looked like in 3-D!" Guisewite exclaimed. Even the jar's hard to fire gold earrings came out well, despite the illustrator's initial skepticism.

Gold Signature Limited Edition
Mc Me Productions would like you to meet Cathy our new cookie jar.
Cathy is an original design. Upon Cathys approval her creator Cathy Guisewite signed the clay model.
Cathy stands an adorable 11 1/2" high and weighs in at a healthy 5 lbs.
Cathy is lovingly hand painted and finished with the finest ceramic paints and glazes available.
Cathy is proud to be produced entirely in Southern California.
Cathy is numbered and limited to 5000.
Produced by and available from Mc Me Productions under license of Cathy Guisewite Studio.

MC ME PRODUCTIONS • 3428 LEORA ST. • SIMI VALLEY, CA 93063 • (805) 583-2850

Cathy® character jar sculpted by Shi Yi Chen, edition of a few hundred, 1994, $150-175.

Treasure Craft next made a Trigger jar for McMe, sculpted by Roger and Sarah Sun. Roy Rogers was enough taken by the rendering of his faithful horse that he signed his approval—this time, on the front of the bust. Approximately 700 Trigger jars were made by Treasure Craft; Trigger has remained the only Treasure Craft mold still produced by McMe, which had the blocks, cases, and molds for all the other editions destroyed.

Star Jars

As McMe Productions concocted new designs, other cookie jar fans also enjoined the firm to produce limited editions. This was an ironic turnaround for Treasure Craft, which had started a half-century earlier by selling designs it contracted other potters to make.

The *Wizard of Oz®* series created by Treasure Craft for Star Jars was perhaps the largest set of cookie jars ever created. Chen's interpretation of *Dorothy and Toto®* constituted a single, massive two-lidded jar; other major characters like the *Tin Man®*, *Scarecrow®*, *Glinda®*, and the *Wicked Witch®* were offered in editions of 1939, commemorating the year the film hit the big screen. Equally interesting were the smaller editions, including *Winged Monkey®* and the *Mayor®*, which comprised as few as 525 pieces each. The editions sold fast.

Major Oz characters have recently sold from $225-350, with the Dorothy and Toto® jar and other characters in the $150-180 range.

Chen sculpted many of Star Jars' *Wizard of Oz®* jars, the largest line of limited edition characters undertaken. Major characters sold in editions of 1939, others as few as 525. Scarecrow®, $300-365.

Don Winton

Don Winton sculpted his final Treasure Craft cookie jar in 1994, selected by cookie jar collectors and authors Fred and Joyce Roerig to honor the 50th anniversary of *Smokey the Bear*. Winton's 450 seated Smokey jars were followed by a Smokey bust jar the following year. Also in 1995, Mardi Gras Records ordered an edition of 500 of their *Grand Marshal*, leading the Olympia Brass Band through New Orleans.

As McMe Productions returned with new designs in 1995, the tenor had changed at Treasure Craft. Richard Rubin, now Compton's Vice-President, flatly stated: "You are our competition," Lonna McGee-Meyer remembered.

Smokey the Bear anniversary jar, Don Winton's last Treasure Craft jar, edition of 450, 1994, $250-300.

Cookie Jarrin' also commissioned a Smokey bust in 1995.

154   Limited Edition Cookie Jars: 1991-1995

Gallery Editions and Moving Offshore

In truth, Pfaltzgraff's managers did see limited edition cookie jars as a promising future for Treasure Craft. Their *Gallery Edition* became a house line of jars made in quantities of 1000, and the new *Pluto® in Doghouse* jar had obvious appeal. But the new jar didn't get far into production before Pfaltzgraff announced that all production would be shifted to Mexico or China. Curt Blanchard, a 1960s-era designer for Holt Howard, had experience with offshore production, and was hired to quickly move certain molds abroad for continued production.

Though a thousand Plutos were promised, far fewer were made before production shifted to Mexico in September 1995.

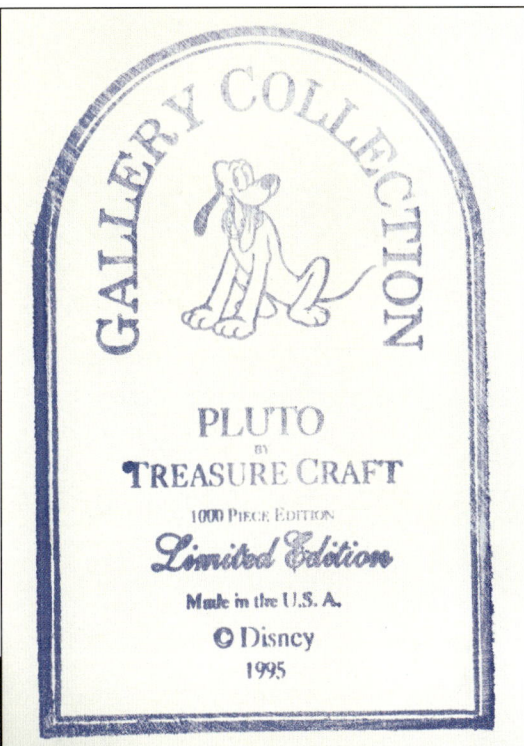

The remaining companies under contract for Treasure Craft limited editions were wildly unimpressed with the quality of the proofs they received. "They had major quality problems as the move to Mexico ensued," confirmed Bill Hamburg of Happy Memories Productions, who'd just hired Treasure Craft to produce busts of *Hopalong Cassidy* and *James Dean*. Only a few jars were ready when the California plant closed; after demanding the return of the molds, Happy Memories began their own production to fill the 500-piece editions. McMe Productions had the same response, and only six paint samples of their *Gene Autry* cookie jar were made by Treasure Craft's Garcia.

The Gallery Collection continued to be made abroad by Pfaltzgraff under the Treasure Craft name, with a small series of character limited editions running through the late '90s. Import laws required that all Treasure Craft offshore jars be marked with their country of origin; even the handful whose molds originated from Compton now bore a MEXICO or CHINA ink stamp, often applied on the inside rim of their lids. Within a few years, they too went out of production.

Pluto® in the Doghouse, Treasure Craft's first in-house limited edition, 1995, $225-275.

Happy Memories hired Treasure Craft to sculpt masters for James Dean and Hopalong Cassidy jars in Compton. Dissatisfaction with the new offshore decorators meant only a handful of color proofs were made by Treasure Craft.

McMe Productions chose to pull their Trigger mold and make it in-house after Treasure Craft moved offshore. Treasure Craft (left) used darker grey wash than the McMe example (right), $200-250.

Roy Rogers would be the last celebrity to sign a Treasure Craft mold, 1995.

Limited Edition Cookie Jars: 1991-1995   157

How Treasure Craft Was Made

There were many different ways to form, fire, and decorate pottery pieces. As Treasure Craft moved through time, their machinery and methods became more sophisticated.

This guide to pottery production is an attempt to express, in lay terms, how these pieces came to be. While not a scientific view of all the workings of a pottery plant, it's hoped this will bring appreciation of the labor of the hundreds of employees who made Treasure Craft over fifty years of production.

Step 1: The Design and Master Mold

Ideas often came right from Al Levin's sketchbooks, or from the drawings of art directors and sculptors in later years.

From the sketch was sculpted a wax model, rendering the final product's shape. The mold shop would then cast artist's clay around the wax model, keeping it moist so it wouldn't adhere. This resulted in a negative image in two or more parts.

Plaster of Paris would be poured into the mold parts and allowed to harden. This would be carved and details added, making an identical likeness to the pieces to be produced. Master molds were thus created; these costly masters were generally kept in a safe area in case of theft, fire or earthquake.

Initial design ideas often came right from Al Levin's sketchbooks.

Step 2: Production Molds

One of a handful of surviving master molds is 1958's Matador.

The master mold was soaped, and hydrocal poured around it to form a die. The die would be separated into its parts, the soap acting as an agent so it could be removed. From the die, production molds were formed; some could make just one item at a time, but smaller, flatter items (such as Handi-Trays) came from stacking dies that could cast four pieces simultaneously.

Each production mold was good for several hundred uses, until the abrasion of the clay running into the molds wore away too much detail. (This is why collectors have noticed that some Treasure Craft pieces have crisper detail than other identical pieces.)

Step 3: Mixing the Clay

Treasure Craft was made of California clays with additional ingredients from other states, including barium carbonate, soda ash, sodium silicate and talc. The ingredients were blended on site in huge water tanks by a large mechanical blade. Hoses hooked up to the tanks were used to spray the plaster-like clay formula into the molds.

Mario carves a production mold for Justice Designs in the shop where he first learned to carve for Treasure Craft.

Step 4: Forming the Piece

Cipriano removes cast clay from the mold.

Pieces could be formed various ways. In Treasure Craft's earliest days, elfin creatures were cast in crude dies, and feet appear to be hand-formed so the piece would stand flat.

Slip casting was the way most three-dimensional Treasure Craft pieces were formed until the 1970s. Liquid clay slip would be poured into the die, slowly hardening from the outer edge. When the wall of the ware (such as the sides of a Sprite wall pocket) had hardened to sufficient thickness, the mold would be removed, and the excess slip poured from the inside of the piece back into the clay tank.

Only a few pieces per day could be made using slip casting methods. As demand grew, Treasure Craft brought in new ram presses, machines that could press a hydrocal die into a block of clay. This was suitable for trays, platters, and other two-dimensional pieces, and could produce 100 times more pieces per day than slip casting could.

But bowls, canisters, and other deep items couldn't be made by ram presses, since the heat caused by 60 tons of hydraulic pressure would scratch and warp the dies. Around 1980, Pottery Craft's jiggering machine came to be shared by Treasure Craft; this machine spun the dies so that the clay was thrown vertically (similar to a potter's wheel), rather than smashed into shape. As long as the sides of the item didn't narrow at the top, the dies could be lifted straight out so slip casting wasn't required. This allowed 500-1000 pieces to be made daily, as opposed to three or four per day using slip casting methods.

Step 5: Finishing

When items came out of hinged molds, seams remained where the molds met. These seams were smoothed by finishers so as not to interrupt the shape or pattern of the piece. Finishers also smoothed out other rough spots or minor imperfections before the piece was fired and decorated.

Finishers also applied pieces together for completion as needed. Sprites were stuck to planters, nameplates were stuck to souvenirs, and the arms of hula girls were applied with small amounts of liquid slip, then finished so no lines showed.

Finishers polish away mold residue before firing.

Step 6: Firing and Decorating

Decorators at Justice still hand rub some finishes.

Treasure Craft's earthenware was fired for approximately five hours at cone 05-06, around 1800 degrees Fahrenheit. (This compares with Pottery Craft stoneware and porcelain, which fired at a much hotter cone 5-9, or 2400 degrees F.) The result was a pure white bisque piece, which was sent to decorate after cooling.

Decorating was done many ways at Treasure Craft. The first step was to determine if any parts were to be left undecorated on the first pass; Mrs. Stewart's Bluing® was used to keep the faces of Sprites bare, and was used on later figurines and tableware to keep colored and crackle glazes out of any areas to be rubbed with wood stain later. If an item needed to be vitreous, it often was fully dunked in the colored glaze (this is why the bottoms of Sprite planters are also glazed in solid colors).

Underglaze paint and decals were also applied at this point (for example, the rubber-stamp applied chili peppers on Taos dinnerware); a clear gloss or matte overglaze would then cover the entire piece so the color would melt and seal during firing.

After the final firing, pieces annealed and cooled for around twenty-four hours. Ware that needed additional decorating was hand-painted (as in the case of Sprite facial features, or the gold leaf hats on the mouse musicians). Wood stain finishes were mixed in a fifty-five gallon drum and rubbed on by hand, then sealed with a lacquer spray.

Step 7: Out the Door!

Larger pieces were hand packed in boxes, smaller ones skin packed after machines were procured in the 1960s. Treasure Craft logo cartons, stamped with their initial destinations, have sometimes survived to protect items for today's collectors.

Salomi Brown working over the wood stain barrel in the Hawaiian plant, c. 1970s.

Five decades of wire makers and assemblers have worked at the Compton pottery plant.

160   How Treasure Craft Was Made

Marks, Labels, and Back Stamps

In the early days, Treasure Craft left the factory unmarked as often as not, or their paper labels were washed off by their new owners. But by the late '50s, Treasure Craft understood that marking every item helped establish their name, reducing confusion for modern-day collectors.

While each maker of a production mold might subtly vary marks carved into the molds, this compendium should chronicle most demarcations collectors have discovered.

Early Marks, Gardena and South Gate

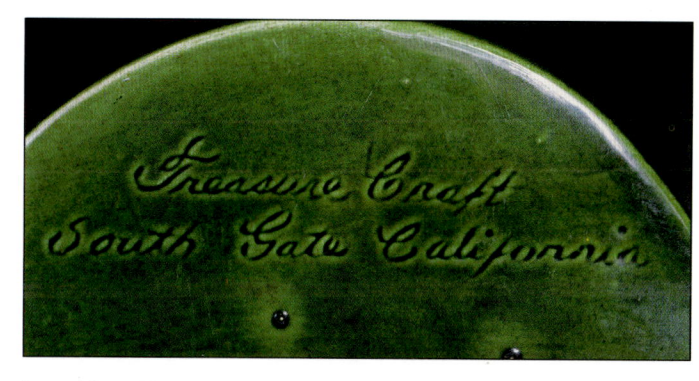

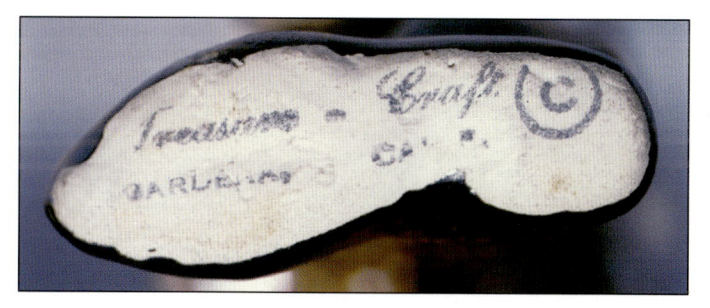

The earliest known mark, the Gardena ink stamp, 1947-1948 only.

In-mold mark on pieces made in the South Gate factory in the early '50s.

Foil treasure chest label, 1951-1956.

South Gate ink stamp, 1949 to early '50s.

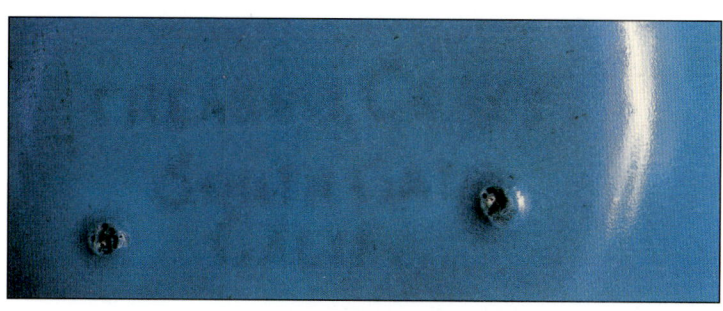

Late South Gate embossed mark, c. 1955.

Paper label, c. 1950.

Ink stamp on new South Gate lines, 1956 only.

Tiny round Registered California label occasionally found on Treasure Craft, c. 1951.

Hawaiian Marks and Labels, 1959-1984

Date reflects mold copyright only…Hawaiian production ensued in 1959.

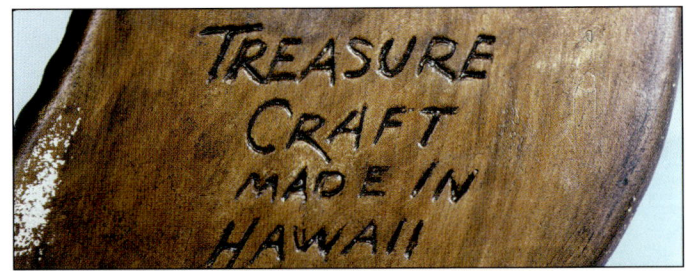

Early Beachwood mark doesn't indicate maker, c. 1959.

Clarence De Coite's early hand-scratched mark raised sales 10%, was stylized into later Hawaiian molds.

Tapa mark on some early bordered pieces, c. 1959.

Scarcely seen die stamp mark with Al Levin's initials, 1963.

162   Marks, Labels, and Back Stamps

Scroll-type mark, adopted late 1960s.

Pottery Craft Marks, 1973-1985

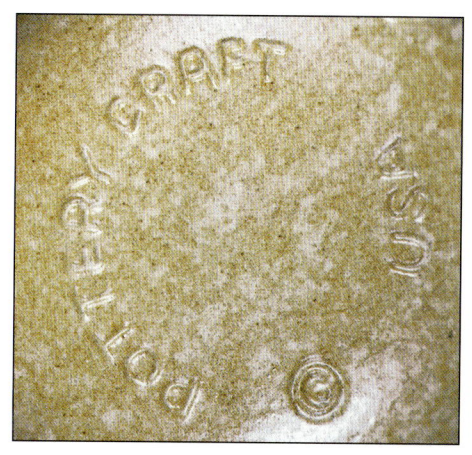

Pottery Craft in-lid mark.

Full mark on Clay Menagerie tray, late '70s.

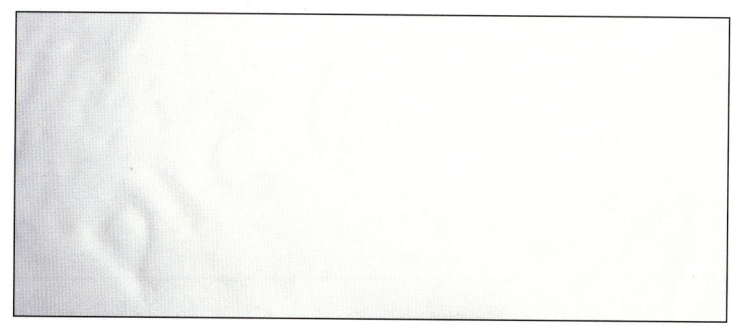

Oval foil Made in Hawaii label, used most years.

PIC mark on small items reflects mistaken impression that '70s trademarks required three letters.

TIC©HAWAII mark, '70s.

Scarce advertising mark without maker's mark, c. 1970.

Pottery Craft foil label.

Marks, Labels, and Back Stamps 163

Compton Marks, 1955-1995

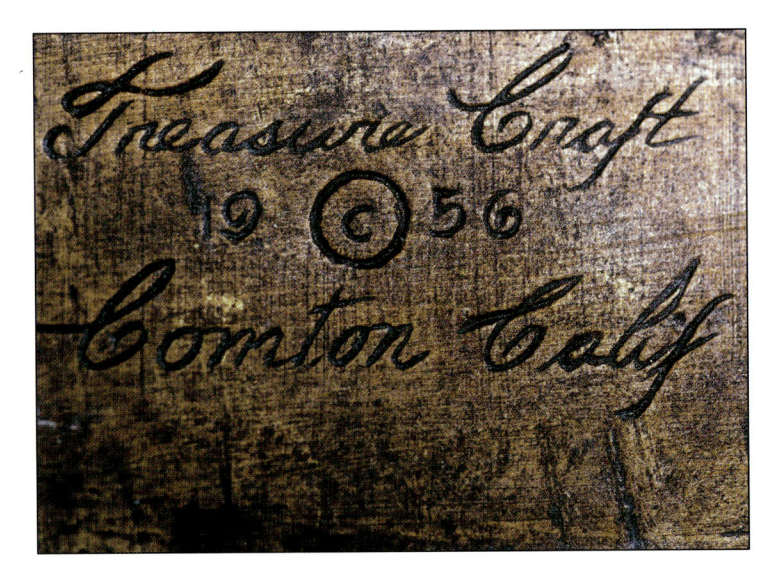

Early "Comton" mark, 1956.

Transition from South Gate to Compton left occasional marks without maker's name.

Script mark under mug edge, 1958.

Mark on back of figurine base, '50s.

USA date mark, 1960s.

Scroll/Disney mark, early 1970s.

Side-by-side comparison of Tiki gods shows adjustments between mainland and Hawaiian molds.

164　Marks, Labels, and Back Stamps

Made in America sticker, often added in 1970s.

Crafted with Pride in America backstamp, 1980s-'90s.

Stylized base mark on Raoul Coronel styled vases.

Pattern name backstamp, 1980s-'90s.

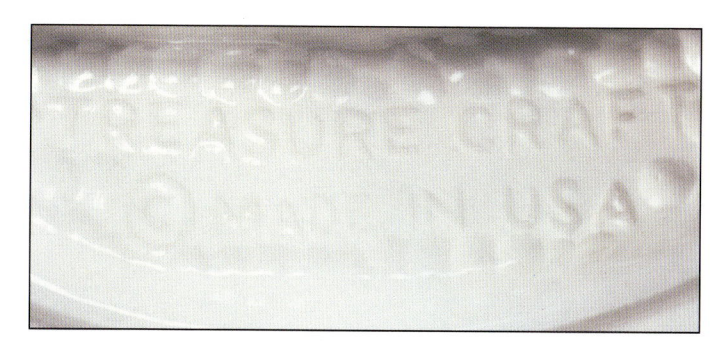

Under lid mark on later cookie jars.

Oval foil label, 1960s-1985.

Marks, Labels, and Back Stamps 165

Look-Alikes

Treasure Craft was both market leader and market follower at different points in its history. As such, many items have been attributed to them in error…contrary to accepted truth, they did not make every piece of 1960s wood stained pottery! And much of Treasure Craft's production before wood staining has mistakenly been credited to other makers.

While a study of the items and marks shown in this book provide the best clues to identifying Treasure Craft, this short review of some look-alike pieces should help collectors narrow their search.

Pixies, Elves, and Other Non-Sprites

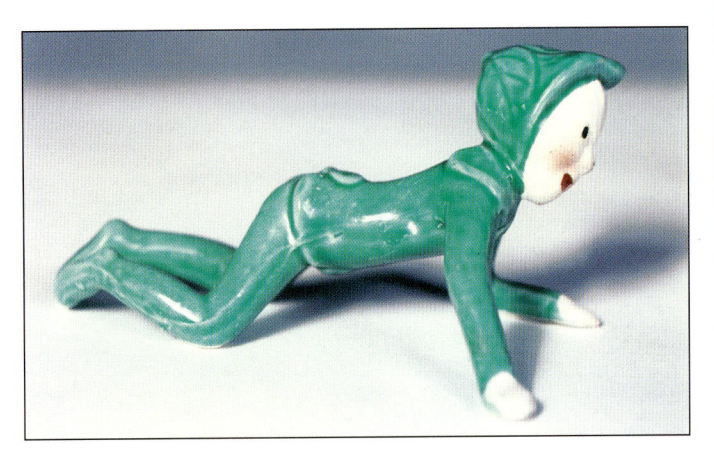

Arcadia Ceramics elf shakers on stump are fully glazed, unlike Sprites.

Pixie Potters crawler, the granddaddy of all other California elves, c. 1940.

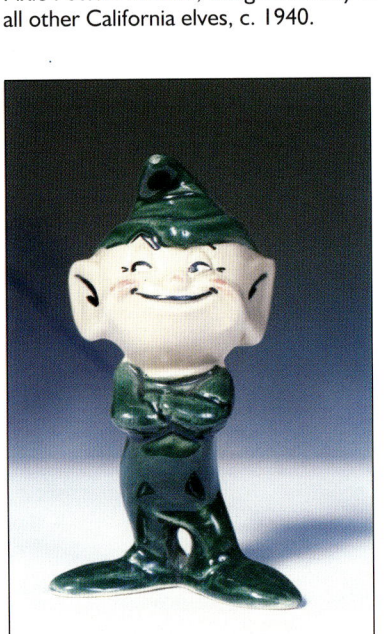

Gilner and others set elf figures on similar wares, but overglazing and lack of impressed ears tell the difference.

Doodit by Gleason of L.A., 1951, shows no exposed bisque.

Brayton Laguna Figurines

Brayton Laguna goat, c. 1955. Striated surfaces and evenly dark brown stain distinguish Brayton pieces from Treasure Craft.

Hawaiian and Tropical Knockoffs

Hula dancers, c. 1950s, unknown maker. Painted details are giveaway.

Japanese attempt at Tiki mug, 1960s. Stain is flat and monochromatic compared to Maui pieces.

Look-Alikes 167

Multiple colors on wood stain tell that this piece is Japanese.

California rival Santa Anita Ware's butterfly demonstrates difficulty in blending variegated glazes.

Also of California, Freeman-McFarlin employed a light brown version of wood stain.

168   Look-Alikes

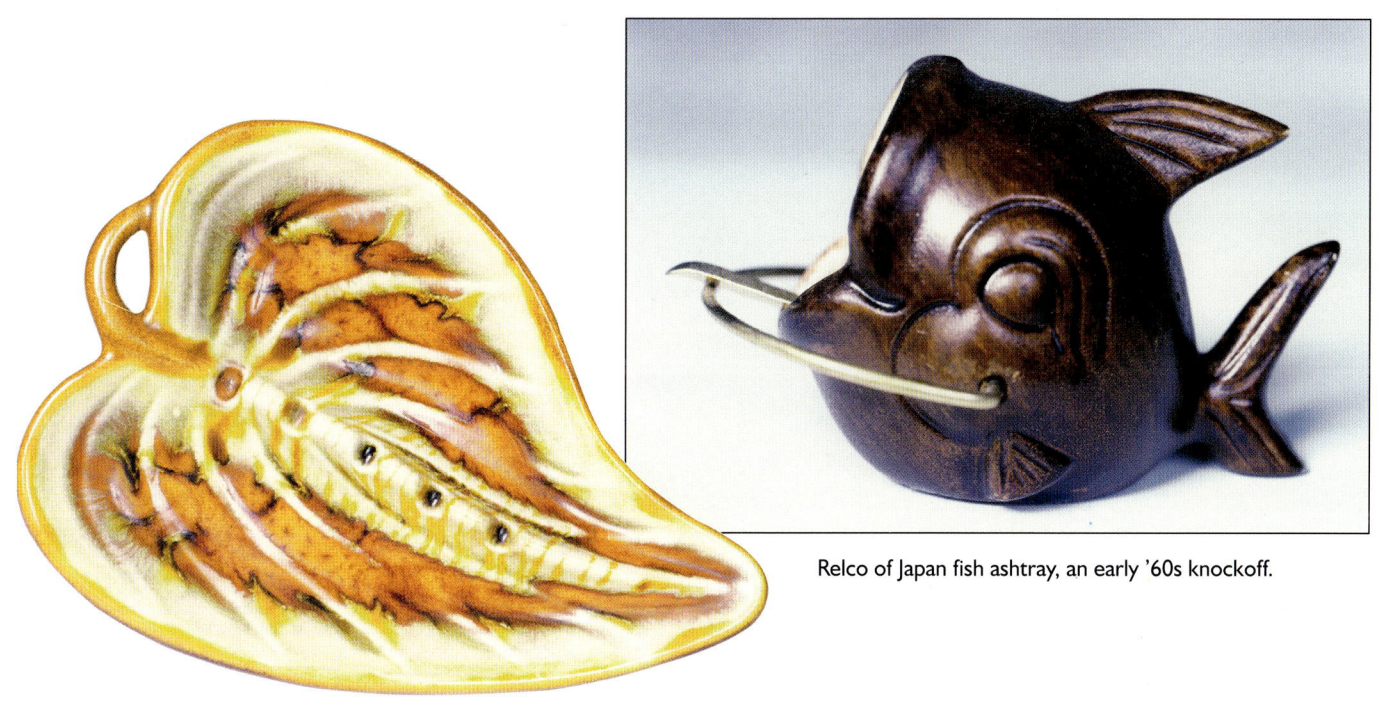

Relco of Japan fish ashtray, an early '60s knockoff.

Maddux of California knockoff of Treasure Craft leaf ashtray has harsher color gradation and no wood stain.

Ray Murray and Tiki Isle

Ray Murray's Hana Isle and Tiki Isle pottery made little fruit trays similar to those he helped design at Treasure Craft of Hawaii, mid-'60s.

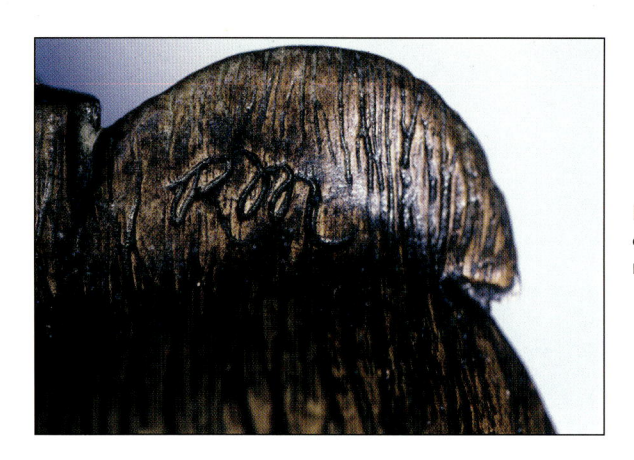

Ray Murray's initials on back of Apple mini-bowl.

Murray made simpler, smaller versions of the Lei Footprint tray he'd designed for Treasure Craft.

Back marks of Murray's post-Treasure Craft footprints.

Hawaiian Fantasies

Hawaiian Fantasies pineapple tray made from Treasure Craft mold, 1994 and '95 only.

Tableware and Cookie Jars

Please don't call it "Treasure Chest"! That name belonged to a Canadian importer of Japanese dinnerware.

Maurice of California owl cookie jar shows uniformity of their medium brown stain. Twin Winton and California Originals jars can be similarly differentiated from Treasure Craft; cold painting over the surface is another clue.

Cal Style (California Originals) glazes weren't controlled in the same way as Compton's.

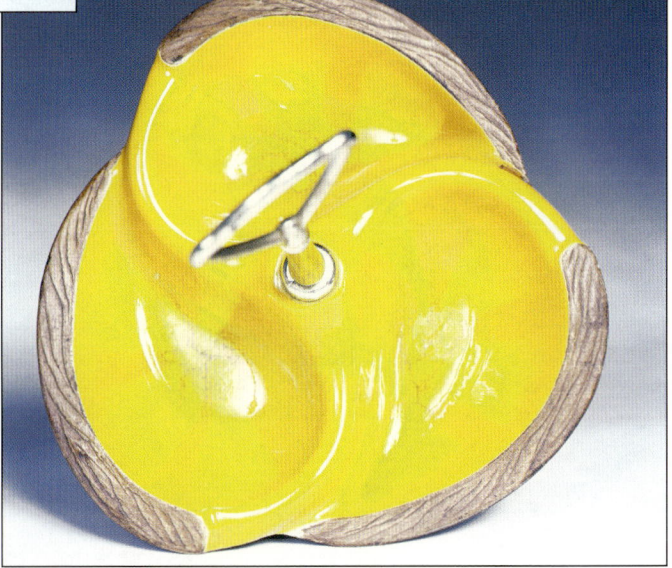

American Bisque of Ohio's wood bark accessories were called "Sequoia Ware," with only a squarish mold number marked on them, never the maker's name. Note the even color and lack of highlighting compared to Treasure Craft glazes.

Look-Alikes 171

Treasure Craft Alumni

It took hundreds of workers over five decades to turn the visions of Treasure Craft's owners and designers into the fun and functional pottery people still enjoy. We pay tribute to their work, and dedicate this remembrance to them all (type of work done shown in parenthesis):

Conrado Acosta (press); Juan Acosta (press); Socorro Acosta (finish); Concepcion Aguilar; Jose Aguilar; Estela Aguirre (sorting); Consuelo Alvarez (production office); Graciela Alvarez (decal); Luis Alvarez (shipping); Cissy Alvaro (customer service); Miguel Anaya (mold shop); Guadalupe Andrade (spray); Stella Anibab (sales); Ruben Arenas (shipping); Perfecto Arredondo; Victor Arredondo (kilns); Yolanda Avalos (product development); Jon Bassi (mold shop); Benigno Baez; Bertha Baez; Edwin Baker (maintenance); Tony Baker (maintenance); Lidia Barragan (decoration); Raul Barragan (kilns); Amalia Barrera (decoration); Regine Beauvoir (secretarial); Eva Bego; Luiz Bego; Luis Bejar (kilns); Lourdes Bernal (finish); Ana bolero; Karen Bonde (product development); Daniel Boone (maintenance); Guadalupe Boone (decoration/press); Alfonso Botello (kilns); Otilio Botello (glaze); Samuel Botello (casting/kilns); Joyce Brinks (secretarial); Harold Brittain; Salomi Brown (decoration); Mark Bruhns (sales); Alejandro Bueina; Josefina Burgos (production office); Pedro Burgos (molds and dies); Bob Burk (manager); Don Bustead (ceramic engineer); Felipe Cabrera; Esteban Camacho (maintenance); Josefina Camacho (finish); Martin Camacho (casting); Josefina Camarena; Tom Campa (product development); Art Caracoza (purchasing); Albino Carillo (manager); Antonio Carillo; Ascencion Carillo (casting); Elpidio Carrillo (casting); Faustino Carrillo (chipping); Guadalupe Carrillo (decoration); Jorge Carrillo (expeditor); Julia Carrillo (finish); Lucila Carrillo; Micaela Carrillo (finish); Olga Carrillo (production office); Ramona Carrillo; Rosario Carrillo (finish); Tim Carter (computer manager); Caroline Calasa (plant manager); Ignasia Casarez (packing); Pablo Castellanos; Xochilt Casteneda (product development); Leticia Cazares (decoration); Adrian Centeno (glaze); Jazmin Cerna (decoration); Carmela Cervantes; Irma Cervantes (decoration); Silvia Cervantes; Charlie Chandler (office); Hank Charney (office); Alicia Chavez (decal); Jun Chen; Shi Yi Chen (sculptor); Guadalupe Chavez (production office); Herminia Chavez (finish); Jose Santos Chavez (kilns); Santos Chavez (glaze/kilns); Azencion Chonita; Elvin Christenson; Rose Clark (office); Rosalva Clemente (purchasing); Maria Con (decoration); Lucila Contreras (decoration); Ruben Contreras (shipping); Maria Cornejo; Morena Cornejo; Pablo Cornejo (packing); Emilio Corono; Karen Cronvich (sales); Asuncion Cruz; Lucas Cruz; Friselda Cuthbert (personnel); Jeffrey Cuthbert (maintenance); Jim Davis (sales manager); Rick Davis (press supervisor); Clarence De Coite (plant manager); Susana de Dios; Elvia Dias (production office); Deborah Diego; Jay Ditmar (maintenance); Leo Dix (production manager); Johnny Dixon (chief of maintenance); Fausto Dominguez (security); Nina Dooley (director of product development); Rafael Durazo (material handling); Jim Ecker (purchasing); William Edsall (plant engineer); Linda

A third of the staff of Justice Designs are veterans of Treasure Craft. Some have worked in the Compton plant for more than a quarter-century.

Escobido (order processing); Joel Esparz; Maria Esther Espinoza; Maria Espitia; Salvador Espitia (kilns); Teresa Espitia; Maria Espitia; Bashir Farhad (production office); Georgina Fernandez; Pocho Fernandez; Daniel Fierro (production manager); Asuncion Figueroa; Orlando Franada (glaze); Antolina Franco (finish); Karen Franco; Felisa Franco (finish); Masakazu Fujii (plant manager and designer); Maria Galindo; Arturo Garcia (glaze engineer); Claudio Garcia; Gina Garcia; Ramon Garcia; Raquel Garcia; Bertha Garnica; Allison Gibson-George (sales); Carmen Gomez; Esperanza Hope Gomez (decoration); Rosey Gomez (samples); Alejandro Gonzalez; Amparo Gonzalez; Consuelo Gonzalez (decal); Francisco Gonzalez (decoration supervisor); Guadalupe Gonzalez (spray); Guillermina Gonzalez; Jose Gonzalez (maintenance); Josefina Gonzalez (finish supervisor); Luiz Gonzalez; Rosalva Gonzalez (spray); Tito Gonzalez (mold shop case maker); Steve Grant (director of administration); Joe Green (decoration supervisor); Carmen Guardardo (production office); Jesus Guardardo (packing); Tony Guerrero (art director); Maria Guillen; Cristina Gutierrez (finish); Elvira Gutierrez (packing); Maria Gutierrez (packing); Maria C. Gutierrez; Guadalupe Guzman; Elizabeth Han; Doris Heisner (secretarial); Cipriano Hernandez; Esteban Hernandez; Irma Hernandez; Jose Hernandez (glaze); Lidia Hernandez; Maria Hernandez; Maria de Jesus Hernandez; Maria G. Hernandez; Melania Hernandez (press); Ofelia Hernandez; Raul Hernandez; Santos Hernandez; Sebastiano Hernandez; Victoria Hernandez; Ron Herro (finance director); Blanche Hew; Avril Higgins (secretarial); Gert Himes (stain supervisor); Ray Hunt (maintenance manager); Anna Iwasikwa (finish supervisor); Arturo Jimenez (mold shop); Rosario Isabel Jimenez (payroll); Ruth Jo (accounting); Earl Johnson (health and safety manager); Kohi Kato (modeler and designer); Mayumi Kato (modeler and designer); Inez Kekula; Inez Kekula II; Kim Kellum (secretarial); Dale Kennedy (office manager); Scott Kingstand (sales manager); Gene Klunk (controller); Lenora Klunk (office); Lorraine Law (customer service); Russ Law (production manager); Benigno Leon (casting); Al 'Boss' Levin (founder/chairman); Brandon Levin (production/glaze); Bruce Levin (Pottery Craft founder, president/CEO of Treasure Craft); Irving Levin (shipping); Jeanette Levin (shipping/secretarial); Jolene Levin (office); Ryan Levin (office); Susan Levin (consumer service); Carlos Linares (casting conveyor/union president); Amalia Lopez (decoration); Consuelo Lopez; Estela Lopez (packing); Javiar Lopez (press/jigger); Rosa Lopez (decoration); Manuel Lucero (casting); Maria Lucero (decal); Paul Lumpkins (jigger); Elvia Luna; Enedina Luna; tom Lynch (accounting); Alicia Macias (samples); Carmen Macias (decoration); Rebeca Macias (finish); Mark Mackanic (accounting); Adolfo Madrigal (supervisor); Octavio Madrigal (production manager); Raul Madrigal (glaze/material handling); Maria Maldonado; Flora Martin; Tim Martin (plant manager); Vince Martinez (modeler/designer); Robert Maxwell (modeler/designer); Manuel Mejia; Mickie Mendez (purchasing); Ismael Meza (casting); Jesus Meza; Luis Meza; Paz Meza (finish); McGowan Michael (sales manager); Lupe Millan (product development); Mario Millan (modeler/master tool maker); Masami Monden (press supervisor); Albino Montes (shipping); Brijido Montes (casting); Genoveva Montes (finish); Jorge Montes; Jose Montes (casting); Merced Montes (casting); Rafaela Montes (finish); Ramon Montes (casting); Rosa Montes (packing); Teresa Montes (decoration); Imelda Moran (decoration); Irene Moreno (finish); Lupe Moreno (shipping); Mercedes Moreno (shipping); Janice Moniz-Tanabur (sales); Hisako Mukai; Don Mulliken (sales); Chuy Murillo (packing); Esperanza Murillo; Maria Murillo (decoration); Ray Murray (plant manager/designer); Frances Nascimento (finish); Alicia Ortiz; Mario Ortiz; Mario Padialla (decal); Ana Padillo; Dolores Padillo; Guadalupe Palacio; Randy Palmer (accounting); Consuelo Parra (packing); Martin Parra (mold shop); Denise Pasquaye (computer manager); Robert Pasquaye (controller); George Patel (decoration); Adriana Perez; Bertha Perez (production); Eladio Perez (mold shop); Elva Perez; Eracleo Perez (mold shop); Juana Perez; Lourdes Perez (customer service); Lucina Perez; Nelba Perez; Sam Perez (sales); Mary Perreira; Mary Jo Phillips (office); Tom Phillips (VP-manufacturing); Guadalupe Pinedo (decoration); Dennis Poppe (sales manager); Annette Psyck (plant manager); Artemisa Quintana (decoration); Ema Quintana (decoration); Emma Quintana (decoration); Rosa Ramirez (finish); Carmen Reyes (decoration); Jose Reyes (shipping); Luz Reyes (decoration); Ricardo Reyes; Amelia Rios (finish); Conception Rios (finish); Irene Rios; Maria Rios (finish); Maria Luisa Rios (finish); Rosa Rios; Sebastiana Rios; Silvia Rios (finish); Leticia Rocha; Maria Rocha (decoration); Mario Rocha; Angelica Rodriguez (decoration); Carmen Rodriguez; Jose Rodriguez; Maria Rodriguez; Maria C. Rodriguez; Maria Luisa Rodriguez (finish); Sandra Rodriguez; Candelaria Rojas (decoration); Consuelo Rojas; Jesus Rojas (shipping); Juana Rojas; Consuelo Rosas (finish); David Rosas (kilns); Rosario Rosas (press); Imelda Becerra Rubin (secretarial); Noemi Rubin (sample coordinator); Richard Rubin (VP-manufacturing); Francisco Ruiz (warehouse); Maria Ruiz (production office); Refugio Ruiz (production office); Saida Ruiz (decoration); Victor Ruiz; Zaida Ruiz (decoration); Maria Sagrero (decoration); Esteban Samudio; Victor Samudio; Alfonso Sanchez (kilns); Bertha Sanchez; Ramon Sanchez (casting); Enedino Sandoval; Amparo Sawada (decoration); Toshiaki Sawada (assistant plant manager); Janet Scheer Parks (product development director); Dirck Schou (general manager); Al Schulman (VP-sales); David Segura (shipping); Joe Segura (shipping); Lucy Segura (packing); Lee Shank (plant manager); Aaron Shayne (sales); Doreen Shimizu (office); Shou-I Sun (modeler/designer); Kimie Tanaka; Maria Tellez; Mark Thomas (office); Wendy Tok (accounting); Irene Vazquez; Ruben Vazquez; Sharon Vegas; Ben Watanabe (sales); Nancy Watanabe (office); Amy Way (designer/product development manager); Emestina Wenceslao (finish); Manuela Wenceslao; Maria Wenceslao (decal); Rosa Wenceslao (production office); Rosario Wenceslao (finish); Tomas Wenceslao (casting); Helen Whyte (ordering manager); Alex Wittner (sales manager); Antonio Zambrano (mold shop); Carmen Zambrano (finish); Guadalupe Zambrano (decal); Ismael Zambrano; Juan Zambrano (jigger); Rosalva Zambrano; Tony Zambrano (kilns); Victor Zambrano (kilns/material handling); Esteban Zamudio (mold shop); Felix Zamudio; Genoveva Zamudio (finish); Art Zerger (assistant plant manager); Luiz Zuniga; Maria Zuniga…

…and all those others whose names are lost with time.

Bibliography

Chipman, Jack. *Collectors Encyclopedia of Bauer Pottery*. Paducah, Kentucky: Collector Books, 1998.

Chipman, Jack. *Collectors Encyclopedia of California Pottery*. Paducah, Kentucky: Collector Books, 1999.

Chipman, Jack and Barbara Willis. *Classic California Modernism*. Venice, California: JaBa Books, 2003.

Cunningham, Scott. *Hawaiian Religion and Magic*. St. Paul, Minnesota: Llewellyn Publications, 1994.

Elliott-Bishop, James. *Franciscan, Catalina & Other Gladding McBean Wares*. Atglen, Pennsylvania: Schiffer Publications, 2001.

James, Van. *Ancient Sites of Hawaii*. Honolulu, Hawaii: Mutual Publishing, 1995.

Janes-Brown, Liz. "Tiki Tacky." *The Maui News*-Currents section, April 6, 2003.

Roerig, Fred and Joyce. *Collector's Encyclopedia of Cookie Jars*. Books I, II & III. Paducah, Kentucky: Collector Books, 1998.

Schaum, Gary V. *Collectors Guide to Frankoma Pottery*. Gas City, Indiana: L-W Book Sales, 1997.

Summers, Catherine. *Material Culture: The J.S. Emerson Collection of Hawaiian Artifacts*. Honolulu, Hawaii: Bishop Museum Press, 1999.

Supnick, Mark and Ellen. *The Wonderful World of Cookie Jars*. Gas City, Indiana: L-W Book Sales, 1995.

Tompkins, Sylvia. *The Collectors' Guide to Salt and Peppers*. Vol. III. Atglen, Pennsylvania: Schiffer Publishing, 2004.

Categorical Index

(illustration page numbers in **bold**)

Alumni/employee list, **172**
Care/Condition, 11-13
Character ware:
    Aladdin, **141**
    Cathy, **125**, **152**
    Country Bear Jamboree, **99**
    Dale Evans, **157**
    Disney (standard), **7**, **138**, **141-143**, **147**, **155**
    Dog Café, **141**
    Droopy, **148**
    Gene Autry, **155**
    Grand Marshal, **154**
    Hopalong Cassidy, **156**
    Jack Skellington, **141**, **142**, **148**
    James Dean, **156**
    Muppets, **143**
    Mrs. Potts, **141**
    Rose Petal Place, 118
    Roy Rogers and Trigger, **150-151**, **157**
    Simba, 7
    The Simpsons, **143**
    Smokey the Bear, **154**
    Wizard of Oz, **153**
Cookie Jars (also see Characters): 8-9, **76**, 79, **79**, 100, **100-101**, **103-104**, 111, 118, 123, 125, **125**, **135-137**, 140, **140-143**, **148-157**
Designers:
    Blanchard, Curt, 155
    Chen, Shi Yi, 123, 125, **125**, **135**, **138**, **140**, **141**, **142**, **152**, 152-153
    Colonel, Raul, 97, **97**
    Dooley, Nina, 122-125, **123**, **140**, **141**
    Ferguson, Scott, 101, **103**
    Fujii, Masa, 108, **109**, 111-114, 119, **119**, **126**
    Green, Bob, 122, **122**
    Guerrero, Tony, 35-40, **36-96 inclusive**, 49-51, 76-79, 97
    Johnson, Rodger, 110, **110**
    Levin, Alfred, 16, **16**, 18, **50**, **78**, **158**
    Levin, Bruce, **99**, 100, 105, **109**, **141**
    McChesney, Susan, 122, **133**, **135**
    Kato, Masami 'Mami', 119, **119**, **126**
    Maxwell, Robert, 98, 105-108, 110; also see Pottery Craft
    Mitsuo, 109, **109**, **115-116**

    Murray, Ray, 52-54, **52-53**, **71**, **169-170**
    Scheer, Janet, 122
    Sun, Roger and Sarah, 122, 153, 157
    Walsh, David, 139, **139**
    Way, Amy, 122
    Winton, Don, **7**, 79, 100, **100-101**, 103, 110, **111**, **135**, **137**
Dinnerware patterns:
    Americana Quilt, 131, **146**
    Avignon, 131, 140, **146**
    Auntie Em series, 122, 130, **130**, 133
    Bandana, **129**, 140
    Blue Mountain, 130, 140, **146**
    Butterfly, **77**, **95**, 101, **101**, 103, 117, 127, **127**
    Cameo Rose, 131, **139**
    Chesapeake, 131, 140, **140**
    Dauphine, 131
    French Village, **130**, **134**
    Garden Party, **138**, **145**
    Midnight Sun, 138, **139**
    Mirage, 121, **121**, **128**
    Paradise Collection, **128**, **129**
    Poppy, 101, 117, **118**, 127, **127**
    Ribbon Geese, 122, **133**
    Rosemarie, 131, 134
    Saratoga, **128**
    Seascape, **123**
    Shenandoah, 131
    Silhouette, 138, **145**
    Southwest, 117, **127**, **128**
    Taos, 110-111, 121, **121**, **127**, **128**
    Tivoli **129**
Figures:
    Chinese line, **39**, **42**, **44**
    Clay Menagerie, **109**, **115-116**
    Cowboy and Stallions, 41
    Colonel bottle vases, 97, **97**, **165**
    Dancers, **37**, **37-38**, **42-43**, 76, **76**; also see Hawaiiana
    Animal designs, 19, **39**, 79, **91**, **98**, **104**, **106**, **107**, 109, **109**, **114-116**
    Elves and Pixies, 14-17, **16**, **32**
    Hawaiian: see Hawaiiana
    Laborers, 59, **78**, **78**
    Lucky California Sprites, **6**, **12**, **18-20**, 19, **26-29**, 34, **34-35**, 45
    Matador and Bull, **8**, **39**, **39-40**, 44, **158**

    Musicians, **17**, **32**, **41**, **44**, **60**
    Naughty Gnomes, 16
    Santa, **9**, **25**, **34**
    Ubangi, 38, **38**, **45**, **57**, **92**
    Wee Wuns, **11**, 19, **30-31**
Gardenware patterns:
    Cache Pots, 99, **99**
    Chinese Birds, **117**, 118
    Dogwood, 118, **119**
    Fashion Vases, 119, **126**
    Harvest Wheat, 118
    Masa Mami, 119, **119**, **126**
    Pottery Craft, **105-114**
    Pueblo, 102, **102**, **139**
    Wire Ware, 40, **40**
Glaze definitions:
    Antique, 100, **100**
    Crackle, 35, **36**
    Experimental, 35, 45, **55-59**, **62**, **89**
    Flame, 77, **78**
    Gold Leaf, **44**
    Heavenly Blue, 77, **85**
    Honey, 97, **98**
    Natural, **102**
    Peacock, **52**, **77**
    Persimmon, **96**, 97
    Red, **76**, **77**
    Tangerine, **77**
    Walnut/Wood Stain, 35, **36**
Hawaiiana
    Advertising, 56, **57**, **72**, **74**
    50th State, 52, **53**, **66**, **71**
    Beachwood, **66**, **162**
    Chinese Line, **42-44**, **53**
    Coconut, 52, **52**
    Dancers and Drummers, **6**, 49, **50-51**, **51-57**, **59-62**
    Dole Kids, 57, **57**, **72**
    Driftwood, 52, **53**, **66**
    Elemakule, **58**, **58-60**
    Fish, **52-26**, **64-66**, **81**
    Hawaiian Pineapple, 54, **54**, **58**, **59**, **64**, **81**, **89**
    Ki'I, 50, **50-51**, 55, **55-56**, **60**, **63**, **74**
    Lauhalu, 52, **71**
    Menehune, 48, 53, **53-54**, 58, **58**, **88**
    Pu pu Trays, **6**, 52, **52**, **58**, **66**, **70**, **87**
    Tapa, 51, **55**, **67-69**, **73**, **162**
    Tiki gods: see Ki'i

Kitchenware patterns:
- Alouette, **132**
- Barrel, 38, **38-39, 46-47, 73, 76**
- Blossoms, **132**
- Carnival, 124
- Cavalier, 82, **82, 89**
- Cook's Nook, **132**
- Country Inns, **132**
- Fish, **7, 80,** 81, **86, 87**
- Fruit, 81, **81, 88**
- Fruitwood, 40, **46**
- Happy Face, 97, **102**
- Horizon, **134**
- Images, **134**
- Leprechaun, **45,** 80, **80, 89-90**
- Linden Ivy, 122, **130**
- Origins, 139, **139**
- Pacifica, **123, 145**
- Provincial, 81, **81, 89**
- Rooster, **48,** 79, 81, **90**
- Sanibel, 142
- Scratch, Ware 19
- Somerset, **144,** 145
- Spaniel, 79, **79**
- Topiary, 82
- Treasure Chest, **90**

Lamps/Lighting:
- Mounted, **33**
- Television, 35-36, **36**

Managers, Owners, Agents:
- Bassi, John, 119
- Casala, Caroline, 55
- Darvill, Edward, 19
- DeCoite, Clarence, 54-57
- Dickson, Johnny, 37
- Fogel, Morey, 53
- Garcia, Arturo, 150
- Helgesen, Paul, 142
- Hunt, Ray, 37
- Kennedy, Dale, 49
- Levin, Alfred, 14-18, **15,** 35-40, 49, **50,** 51-52, 54-56, 58-59, 78-80, 97-100, 105-108, **120**
- Levin, Bruce, 37, 99-101, 106-108, 119-121, 124-126, 139-140, 144, 148
- Levin, Jeanette, 14-18, **15,** 36, **120**
- Murray, Ray, 52-55
- Phillips, Tom, 52, 76
- Psyck, Annette, 55-57
- Rubin, Richard, 154
- Schulman, Al, 19
- Shank, Lee, 35
- Wick, Earling, 50

Manufacturing processes, 159, **159-160**

Media (print):
- Giftwares Magazine, 38
- Los Angeles Times, 141
- Maui News, 49
- Registered California Pictorial, 20, **20**
- S&H Giftbook, 39
- Sundance Catalogue, 124

Movies and television:
- 101 Dalmations, 141
- Aladdin, 141
- Beauty and the Beast, 141
- Friends, 140
- Pinocchio, 138
- Pocohontas, 142
- Snow White and the Seven Dwarfs, 142
- That '70s Show, 111
- The Dick Van Dyke Show, 76
- The Lion King, 7
- The Nightmare Before Christmas, 141, 149
- The Rocketeer, 141
- The Wizard of Oz, 153
- Volcano Joe, 57

Outside organizations:
- Alexander and Baldwin, 49
- Animation, 148
- Barth and Dreyfuss, 122
- Bauer Pottery, 52, 76
- Barbara Willis studios, 35
- Brayton Laguna, 35, 97, **167**
- California Art Potters Association, 17
- California Originals, 118
- Center for Houseware Designs, 122
- Charles Eames studios, 105
- Coco Joe's, 55-56
- Cookie Jarrin', **154**
- Cope Pottery, 15, 18-19
- Dillards, 138
- Ellen Supnick jars, 148, **149**
- Famous Amos, **136**
- Frankoma Pottery, 52
- Gregorian Copper, 15
- Hallmark, 122
- Hana Isle, 54, **169-170**
- Happy Memories, 156
- Hawaiian Fantasies, 58-59, **58, 170**
- Hawaiian Manufacturers Association, 54
- Hawaiian Potters Guild, 49, 51
- Hawaiian Seniors Golf Tourney, 57
- JC Penney, 115, 117, 121, 140
- Justice Designs Group, **36, 144, 159-160, 172**
- Los Angeles Potteries, 49, 56
- Mardi Gras Records, 154
- McMe Productions, 150, **150-152,** 154, 157, **157**
- Mervyns, 121, 139
- Pacific Stoneware (Portland), 106
- Pfaltzgraff, 126, 138-144
- Registered California, 20, **162**
- Robert Maxwell studios, 105-106
- Seattle Worlds Fair, 1962, 54
- Sperry & Hutchinson, 39, 97
- Star Jars, 153, **153**
- Stone Craft, 105-106
- Sultan, 53
- Tiki Isle, 54, **170**
- Tommy Bahamas, 7
- Twin Winton, 100-101
- Walt Disney Productions, 98, 140-141
- Westwood Ceramics, 34
- Williams-Sonoma, 138
- Zak Productions, 143

Pottery Craft:
- Botanical, 108, **111, 114**
- Christmas ornaments, 110, **111**
- Clay Menagerie, 109, **109, 115-116**
- Forest Folk, 110
- Gardenware, **105-107,** 106, 108, **112-114**
- Greetings, **116**
- Jade, **113**
- Kitchenware, **106-114,** 108
- Lamps, 110, **110**
- Maxwell designs, **10, 101,** 105-108, **105-107,** 110, **117, 119**
- Moonstone, **105, 107,** 108, **112**
- Palomino, **107,** 108, **109-113**
- Porcelain animals, **109,** 110, **115**
- Sports figures, **115**
- Sea Mist, **114**
- South of the Border, 110, **111**
- Tierra, **13, 105-109,** 108, **111-112**

Pricing tips, 9-10

Shaker sets:
- Novelty (early), **7,** 17, **17, 21-16,** 34
- Wood Stain, **53, 63, 73, 75, 83, 92-93**
- Pattern matching: see Dinnerware

Souvenirs:
- Advertising, **70-72, 82-83, 96, 162**
- Casinos, **94-95**
- Floridiana, **82, 96**
- Nameplate, 82, **82-83, 86**